EXPLORING THE CATHOLIC CHURCH

EXPLORING THE CATHOLIC CHURCH

HOW BEING A CATHOLIC MAKES A DIFFERENCE TO EVERYDAY LIFE

MARCELLINO D'AMBROSIO

Hodder & Stoughton
LONDON SYDNEY AUCKLAND

First published in Great Britain in 2001, by arrangement with Servant Publications, USA.

10 9 8 7 6 5 4 3 2 1

British Library Cataloguing and Publicaion Data
A record for this book is available from the British Library

ISBN 0 340 78610 8

Printed and Bound in Great Britain by
The Guernsey Press Co. Ltd, Channel Isles

Hodder & Stoughton
A Division of Hodder Headline Ltd
338 Euston Road
London NW1 3BH

Contents

Introduction

Many people view Christianity primarily as a belief system or abstract philosophy. But Christianity is better understood as a story, the story of a relationship. All the major Christian Churches agree on the basics of the story line as recorded in the Bible. Though created for intimate friendship with God, the human race from the beginning chose to go its own way, cutting itself off from its Creator. The misery and death that resulted from this broken relationship could only be overcome by God's initiative. And so God sent his Son Jesus among us in human form. By his act of total self-giving on the cross, Jesus blotted out all human wrongdoing and reconciled us to his Father. By rising from the dead, he liberated us from death's power and offered us a share in God's own inner life, a glorious life that lasts forever. The good news is that this intimate life of union with God through his Holy Spirit is available to all who accept it. So Christianity is not only a story, but an invitation.

Many people have heard this story, often through introductory courses on Christianity such as Alpha, and have accepted the invitation. This book was not written to repeat what such courses do so admirably well. Rather, it was written for people who already understand that Christianity is about personal relationship with God but who wonder about "Catholicism." It is not immediately apparent to many, whether Catholic or not, what devotion to the saints, sacraments, and church hierarchy have to do with an intimate relationship with God in Christ. After all, so many Christians seem to get along fine without these Catholic distinctives.

The purpose of this book is to show that these and other features of Catholic life are neither idolatrous distractions nor optional extras, but valuable gifts intended by God to accelerate our growth in holiness and joy. But unopened presents aren't much use. And for many Catholics, these priceless treasures remain on the closet shelf in their original wrapping paper. So this book is not only an explanation but an invitation to unwrap these gifts and tap into the blessings God makes available through them. To this end, I've offered several practical strategies I've employed over the years to unpack these gifts and unlock their life-changing power for myself and others dear to me.

Jesus wants our joy to be full (see Jn 15:11). He came that we might have life and have it abundantly (see Jn 10:10). The term "catholic" comes from the word "whole." Catholicism is all about the "whole" truth leading to the fullest, deepest, most life-giving relationship with God possible. Why settle for less?

Marcellino D'Ambrosio

Chapter One

Who Needs the Catholic Church?

It was a muggy evening in August, 1971, just a week after my sixteenth birthday. I walked into St. Patrick's Church in Providence, Rhode Island, with no clue that what I was about to experience would change my whole life.

Why church on a Thursday night? Ok, my friends and I were cradle Catholics. But our faith till then had played only a peripheral role in our lives. We were rebels, typical teenagers of the Woodstock era. I, in fact, was well on the way towards a career as a professional rock musician, playing bass guitar in one of the top bands in southern New England.

But two of my friends had suddenly changed. They had caught a glimpse of something more exciting than anything they had ever experienced before, and I had to find out what it was. When I asked my friends to explain the reason for the new glow on their faces, they told me to go to St. Patrick's and find out for myself.

Up to that point, I thought of religion as one of those dull and unpleasant things you had to do in order to avoid more unpleasant things in the future, sort of like saving for retirement. The last thing I expected was that following Christ could provide fulfillment in the present.

But my picture of Christianity was shattered when I walked

into that church basement. Instead of the bored, blank expressions I'd encountered in most congregations, the faces of the five hundred people in this group beamed with joy. As people gathered, the atmosphere was charged with more excitement than I'd seen at any rock concert. No one needed to be cajoled to sing when it was time to begin—the crowd roared as the music group struck up the opening song. After singing their hearts out, they began pouring out exuberant prayers of praise and thanks. Many even got up to tell stories of how Christ had changed their lives and answered prayers in miraculous ways. For these people, God was not a distant monarch, and Christianity was not a matter of rules and regulations. No, God was a loving Father who had given us Jesus as a Savior and the Holy Spirit as the power to make us able to live a new kind of life.

That night, through the love and joy of those people, I met Christ in a more personal way than I could ever have expected. I'd always believed in him, but that night I decided to put him in the driver's seat of my life. As I did so, the Holy Spirit gave me the desire and strength to break out of sinful patterns of behavior that willpower alone had been unable to change.

But along with all these discoveries, a big question arose to confront my friends and me: "Now that we know the Father, Son, and Holy Spirit in a deeper way, why do we need the Catholic Church?" To us, the Church's hierarchy, saints, and traditions seemed a restricting, top-heavy apparatus. "Why not just be solitary, freelance Christians?" we wondered. And some of us did just that.

I wrestled with this question honestly, taking it to God in prayer, taking it to the Bible. And what I discovered was that

God's plan is much bigger than I had imagined and goes far beyond saving isolated individuals.

God's Plan for Unity

Reading Genesis 3, I was struck by the irony of the situation. Here we find Adam and Eve teaming up together against God, but instead of their plot bringing them closer together, it drives them apart. Later, their sons, Cain and Abel (see Gn 4), are so alienated from one another that one actually kills the other. And so the spiral of alienation goes until, with the Tower of Babel, sin causes humanity to fragment into hostile races unable to communicate with each other (see Gn 11).

Stories like this illustrate what sin always does. It alienates and divides people. Jesus came to undo this. He wants not just to save individuals but to repair the harm that sin has done to us as a people. His mission is to bring us together as a united nation, a family, according to God's original intent. The New Testament states this clearly. Jesus died "to gather into one the children of God who are scattered abroad" (Jn 11:52). The letter to the Ephesians says that "the mystery of [God's] will" is now revealed as a plan to unite all things in Christ, "things in heaven and things on earth" (Eph 1:9-10).

This unity is supposed to begin here and now. That's why Jesus created a new community called the church. Just before he died, the Lord offered an impassioned prayer to the Father for his disciples "that they may all be one,... so that the world may know that you have sent me" (Jn 17:21, 23, NRSV). Of course, Jesus' prayer has yet to be fully realized. Creating division and strife in the world is easy; creating unity among different people—that's a miracle of grace. But wherever grace prevails to bring about unity, it proves that Jesus and the power of his Spirit are real.

Following Jesus necessarily means participating in his work of gathering together. As his disciples, we're called to pray and work for unity until Jesus has made us "completely one" with himself and with one another. Once I grasped this, I realized that I couldn't just go my own way. How could I fragment things even more by starting a church with my own friends?

Another aspect of unity arises from the fact that God himself created us in his image and likeness. It dawned on me that God is *community*. He is not a solitary monarch but three Persons in one God. His very essence is a communion of persons.

This has implications for us. It means that, created as we are in the image and likeness of the Triune God, none of us can possibly be happy alone. None of us is sufficient in ourselves or has all the gifts necessary for making our way through life. In order to be faithful to who we are, we must answer the call to be in communion with others. This is part of what God is doing in the church—bringing people into communion with each other so that they can really be themselves.

That means heaven isn't going to be like an office of people, each sitting in a partitioned cubicle, looking at God on a computer monitor. Heaven is going to be a huge party where a big family are together enjoying God and each other as well. Since we're going to be with the church forever, we'd better get used to the idea right now!

What Is the Church?

What *is* the church, anyway? Being rather analytical, I used to be frustrated that I couldn't find a clear definition of the church in the New Testament. I see now that this is because the church is a mystery. The Holy Spirit is the force that binds God's people together as one in the church, and he, being God, eludes the power of our limited minds. You may be able to count how many people attend Sunday Mass, but you can never measure the depth and breadth of the Spirit's activity.

Fortunately, the Scriptures don't leave us clueless. Jesus and the New Testament writers used many *images* to describe the church—ninety-six, according to one scholar. Although we'll examine just a few of those images here, it's important to realize why there are so many: the reality of the church is so big that no single image can possibly do it justice.

Three images in particular helped me understand why I shouldn't try to be a solitary Christian: the church as the *body of Christ*, the *family of God*, and a *holy nation*.

Body of Christ

St. Paul uses this analogy in two of his letters, explaining that members of the church are all "baptized into one body" and are therefore "one body in Christ" (1 Cor 12:13; Rom 12:5). As I thought about this, I had to ask myself: "If the church is Jesus' body, what sense does it make to love Jesus and hate the church?"

Furthermore, as Ephesians 5 points out, Jesus offered his life for the church: "Christ loved the church and gave himself up for her, that he might sanctify her" (Eph 5:25). Jesus loved the church to the point of death.

The body of Christ imagery also helped to correct my view of the church as a static, hierarchical institution where the clergy do everything and the laity just sit around. Wherever this wrong impression came from, it isn't what the Catholic church has ever taught about itself.

The church is a body made up of many members with diverse gifts, as Scripture says in 1 Corinthians 12:4-31. Each member contributes to the proper functioning of the whole body. Certainly, the ordained ministry plays a key role. But for the church to grow and function well, *every* part of the body must contribute its particular gifts and service.

Reflecting on these things, I became aware that, as a member of the church, I need the gifts of others. But this is a two-way street: I have an obligation to put my own gifts at the service of everyone else in the church. I'm needed! I have a role!

Family of God

Scripture's most common image for the church is probably the family. Look at St. Paul's letters, and everywhere you'll find that he calls Christians "brothers and sisters." Other verses speak of the church as "the household of God" (for example, Eph 2:19 and 1 Pt 4:17).

In this family, God the Father is our *Abba* who cares for us and calls us into an intimate relationship with him. Jesus is "the first-born" of our many brothers and sisters (Rom 8:29). The Holy Spirit is the bond holding the family together. And since every family needs a mother, Jesus has kindly shared his mother with us.

In any family, relationships are what it's all about. People marry to have intimacy with each other and with the children God sends them. However, given that we're human beings with bodily needs, our relationships need to be supported by a certain amount of what we'd call institution. We even speak about the *institution* of marriage! Think about it: a married couple has legal status, pays taxes, owns or rents a dwelling, bequeaths its goods to the children and grandchildren. All this is institution at the service of relationship.

That's the way it is with this big family, the church. Although the church is all about relationships, it needs a certain amount of institutional reality to sustain its family life. It's true that there have been many times in Catholic life when institution has been put ahead of relationships. This is unfortunate, but it's the sort of situation that can happen in any family. The problem isn't solved by abolishing the institution. Would you counsel a husband and wife to resolve their marital troubles by getting rid of all their assets? No, you'd tell them to focus on renewing their relationship. The same is true within the church. Instead of firing away at the church as an institution, we need to play our part in renewing the church as family.

Authority is another element of family life that characterizes the church. In a family there are elders, people like grandpa and grandma and Uncle Harry and Aunt Mary who have an important role and a certain amount of clout. You may not always like them, but they have a lot of wisdom to share, and if things are working right, you certainly respect them.

In the church, too, we have elders, ordained leaders who help

God's family to mature and grow. In fact, the word "priest" comes from the Greek word *presbyter,* which means "elder." The priest is an elder brother who carries authority because he has been anointed and gifted to serve us.

We also call our priests "father," a practice that reflects thinking within the early church. St. Paul spoke of his fatherly care for the Corinthians: "For though you have countless guides in Christ, you do not have many fathers. For I became your father in Christ Jesus through the gospel" (1 Cor 4:15). In other letters, too, Paul uses the language of a father-child relationship with the Christians that he evangelized and discipled.

For us today, the person in whom this role of fatherly care and authority is invested most universally is the pope. Interestingly, that's what the very word "pope" means: papa, father. The pope is the father of the entire universal Catholic family, just as the bishop is the father of the diocese, and the pastor and his assistant priests are the fathers of the local parishes.

Special ceremonies are an aspect of family that also figure in the life of the church. I'm talking about occasions like Christmas dinner, where families set the table with the best china and crystal, prepare a special meal, and invite relatives and friends to enjoy it together. Or birthday celebrations, with their obligatory cake and candles and singing of "Happy birthday to you." All these family rituals are important, even those that accompany sad times like funerals. They help a family to express and even to strengthen its bonds.

Likewise, the ceremonies of the Catholic Church are family celebrations. The Eucharist is our family meal, deepening our bonds with the Lord and with each other. Baptism, confirmation, holy orders, and the anointing of the sick—all the sacraments are celebrations that build relationships in the family of God.

Holy Nation

The church can also be described as a people—"a holy nation, God's own people" (1 Pt 2:9). We see in the Old Testament that God intervened in the family of Abraham, Isaac, and Jacob and gradually built it into a nation. It was an imperfect nation (just look at the kings of Israel if you want to see imperfection in leadership). Still it was God's nation.

We, too, are a family grown into a nation whose king, ruler, and Lord is Jesus the Messiah. But we are a *universal* nation, not a particular ethnic group. The word "catholic" means universal, and ever since it first appeared in print—in the writings of St. Ignatius of Antioch, about fifteen years after John's Gospel was written—it has been used as an adjective describing what the church of Christ is meant to be.

Although "catholic" doesn't appear in the New Testament, the reality of what it means is obvious right from the church's very birth at Pentecost. On that occasion, great crowds "from every nation under heaven" were present in Jerusalem, and everyone heard "the mighty works of God" proclaimed in their own language (see Acts 2:5-13). This is also the reality that we will see in heavenly glory. This church triumphant is "a great multitude," impossible to number, "from every nation, from all tribes and peoples and tongues" (Rv 7:9).

Let's explore some of the elements that constitute this nation, the people of God.

History, Heroes, and Holidays

Especially through its schools, a nation makes it a priority to teach its citizens about the great heroes who embody the nation's ideals. In the Catholic Church, the school of the liturgy pays particular attention to the saints, those great heroes and heroines who show us what God's nation is really about and what we're destined to become. Sure, all of us who are Christians are, in a sense, saints. But this is often hard to detect when we look at ourselves and most other Christians we know.

This hit me during a visit to a museum in Florence, Italy, where I saw some unfinished statues by Michelangelo. They were mildly interesting only because I knew who the sculptor was; I breezed by them rather quickly. Then I walked down the hall to where Michelangelo's statue of David was displayed. Wow! Suddenly I understood where the artist was going with those hunks of marble I'd passed by so nonchalantly! After admiring *David*, I rushed back to them and finally could appreciate their noble beauty.

That's the way it is with us and the saints. We're works in progress; the saints are the finished masterpieces who point to what we're called to become. In studying and celebrating their lives, we come to understand our own dignity.

Two thousand years' worth of saints are already in heavenly glory, so we're just the tip of the iceberg, the visible but smaller part of God's "holy nation." Part of what it means to be Catholic, then, is to get to know these many heroes of the faith who have been made holy, perfect, and spotless. We can read their lives and their writings to help us stay on course in running the same race they did. We can keep their statues and pictures around, as other nations do with their heroes. For us, though, such representations aren't just an encouragement to imitation: they're a reminder that the saints are gloriously alive in Christ and that they pray for us.

Nations have holidays. These celebrations of people, exploits, and events bond people together, confer identity, and strengthen unity. Similarly, in the Catholic Church we have holy days that unite us more closely with each other and the Lord, our captain and greatest hero of all. Moving through these yearly celebrations, we enter more and more deeply into Jesus' birth, death, and glorious resurrection.

We celebrate his death and resurrection in a weekly way, too. Every Friday Catholics are called to pray and do penance in some way as we remember Jesus' suffering and our sin, which led to it. On Sunday we rejoice in his Resurrection. It's a festive time to set aside the week's cares and be reminded that we have no really big problems, because Christ is risen and we are free.

The church year also includes a regular cycle of celebrations of its heroes and heroines. Like many Catholics, I especially look forward to the annual remembrances of my favorite saints—Thomas More, Francis and Clare of Assisi—as special days to reflect on their stories and what they mean for my own life.

The Church's Constitution: Not a Dead Letter

A nation needs a constitution. It needs written documents that can serve as a norm for its common life. That's what the Scriptures are in the Catholic Church—this and much more. They are daily nourishment, the ultimate norm of our life and belief. This is why we need to be constantly poring over them.

But even a written document is easily misunderstood. Consider the Constitution of the United States and all the challenges we've had in interpreting it. Well, the Scriptures are open to misunderstanding, too. That's why we need help in grasping their meaning.

We find this help in the Tradition of the Catholic Church. Tradition is the living transmission of the message of the Gospel, the witness and memory of Christ handed down from the first apostles all the way to us in an unbroken succession. Tradition is the native context of the Scriptures that makes them understandable and life-giving for us. This context helps us to answer questions that the Scriptures may not answer directly.

"Brethren," St. Paul advises, "stand firm and hold to the traditions which you were taught by us, either by word of mouth or by letter" (2 Thes 2:15). Here we see that there is no opposition between written Scripture and oral tradition in Paul's mind. Scripture and Tradition fit together naturally, feeding us and providing the guidance we need. They bring us the living word of God.

To Govern Is to Serve

Every nation needs government. Christ knew this, and so he personally chose twelve apostles on whom to establish the church. Why twelve? Because Israel as a nation was founded on twelve patriarchs. Jesus was founding a new Israel, so he chose twelve men and gave them a special responsibility that no one else had.

This unique role stands out both in the Gospels and the Acts of the Apostles, in Jesus' lifetime and afterwards. The apostles were the ones called to serve as the official witnesses of Jesus' resurrection (see Acts 1:22). They were the spokesmen. Together, they were the united body that led the church, and they made important decisions about its direction (see Acts 15:6). The apostles themselves ordained men (see Acts 14:23) that they called bishops (Greek for "overseers"), or presbyters (Greek for "elders"). Those men, in turn, handed on their ministry to others, training them and entrusting to them the ministry of teaching and guiding (see 2 Tm 2:2).

Clearly, it was Christ's intent to provide for an orderly succession of pastors to lead the church. That's what apostolic succession is all about: it's the unbroken chain from Christ to the apostles to their successors through the centuries, down to the present-day bishops of the Catholic Church.

It's important to note that the church doesn't put these men *over* the Bible and Tradition. As the Second Vatican Council noted, these leaders are ***under*** the authority of God's word and are subject to it, like every other follower of Christ (see *Dei Verbum*, par. 10). Their job is to serve the word of God by teaching and interpreting it so that we can take it as the guide of our lives without falling into all sorts of distortions.

For me, this principle was beautifully illustrated at the funeral of Paul VI, one of the twentieth century's greatest popes, the one who had the hard, often unpopular task of completing and implementing Vatican II. On the day of the funeral, a magnificent assembly of dignitaries from all over the world gathered in St. Peter's Square, along with cardinals and bishops in full regalia. It was a bit windy, so hair and ceremonial garb were blowing as the crowd waited. Finally, the casket of Pope Paul VI came into view: a plain pine box, and on top of it, an open book of the Gospels with its pages fluttering in the breeze. What a powerful statement about what leadership in the church is all about! Right there, atop the simple coffin, was the message: the pastors of the church are under the word of God. They are at the service of the word.

Most prominent among these ordained leaders is the pope, the center around whom are gathered all the bishops, successors of the apostles. The pope, as bishop of Rome, is the successor of Peter because Peter was the first leader of the church in Rome and there laid down his life for his sheep in martyrdom.

The apostle Peter was originally named Simon. Jesus changed his name with a word play on the term for rock: "You are Peter, and on this rock I will build my church" (Mt 16:18; see also Jn 1:42). In the Bible a name change always indicates a special destiny, and after this incident we find that Peter does have a unique role. At Pentecost, for example, who but Peter speaks for all the apostles?

Peter is imperfect, as are all the apostles, and Jesus certainly knows about this. In fact, he even predicts that Peter will deny him. At the same time, Jesus promises his special help. "I have prayed for you that your faith may not fail;" he tells Peter, "and when you have turned again, strengthen your brethren" (Lk 22:32). This is Peter's role. Strengthened by Jesus, he strengthens the other apostles and helps maintain their unity. He serves us all by using his authority to bring us to the kingdom. As one of his titles puts it, the pope is truly "the servant of the servants of God."

In a time of particular need in my life, I experienced the charism of the papacy in a poignant way. It happened in Rome in 1975, at the tomb of one of my favorite popes, John XXIII. I had fairly recently catapulted from the world of rock and roll into the Catholic seminary, excited about my faith and wanting to live radically for the Lord. I was also quite judgmental of other seminarians who did not live up to my expectations of what a seminarian ought to be. I knew this was the disdainful spirit of the Pharisee, but I was powerless to change myself. As I prayed at the papal tomb and asked God to change my heart, I felt the gentle presence of John XXIII, who exemplified the love and acceptance of others that I so lacked. This special moment produced such a release of spiritual power that I left a different person. My classmates detected such a change in my attitude that they elected me to represent them in the seminary's student government.

What a wonderful blessing the church is! Far from being the hindrance I once thought it, the church with all its elements—papacy, ordained leaders, sacraments, saints, tradition, brothers and sisters—provides the anchor that keeps us from drifting out to sea with every passing fad.

And in the tempestuous age that we live in, God knows we need an anchor!

Chapter Two

Baptism: Gateway to Life

Catholics certainly seem fond of ceremonies. There are bows and scrapes, pomp and circumstance surrounding every important occasion in Catholic life. This means that anyone who hopes to understand baptism and what it has to do with a personal relationship with Jesus needs to face a more fundamental issue: why do Catholics have *any* rituals at all?

Basically, I've concluded that it has a lot to do with the fact that God gave us bodies! Our bodies provide us with ways to experience God in the world, and they provide God with ways to communicate with us. Speech is one of those avenues, of course, but what I'd especially like to focus on here is the nonverbal language of signs and gestures.

My mother speaks this language especially well. She's Irish, but she lived so long in the Italian cultural environment of the D'Ambrosio family that I call her a born-again Italian. Even when she's driving, Mom can't talk without waving her hands (which is very scary if you happen to be in the passenger seat). If you tied her hands behind her back, she wouldn't be able to communicate!

Generally speaking, we all use gestures to express ourselves. When we meet people, we don't just say, "Hello." We extend our hand or we hug them. If we're French, we kiss them on both cheeks, regardless of sex. The first time I went to Mass in France and a guy turned to kiss me at the sign of peace, I turned a few different shades of red!

Non-verbal communication can be powerful. "Actions speak louder than words," we say. "Talk is cheap. One picture is worth a thousand words." Our Maker is well aware of the impact of various modes of communication, and he uses them all in speaking to us. He addresses us through words but he also communicates through body language. That's what the sacraments are: God's body language. Through the church, his body, God embraces, touches, and blesses us in the sacraments.

I like the fact that the Gospels portray Jesus as expressive and earthy. He doesn't just say "I bless you" to the little children; he takes them in his arms and lays his hands on them (see Mk 10:16). When Jesus heals people, he often touches them. Remember the man born blind, from John's Gospel? Jesus might have cured him with a simple "Be healed." Instead, he spits in dirt, makes a paste, and smears it on the man's eyes. Through the instrument of this mud, the Lord communicates his invisible spiritual power and heals this man (see Jn 9:1-7).

To me, this is a remarkable image of the whole sacramental order. Bread, wine, water, oil—in the life of the church, Jesus uses these very earthy things to transmit something invisible: the life-changing power of God.

Can God's grace come to us outside the sacraments? Absolutely. The Catholic Church has never taught that God's grace is limited to the sacraments. Can God's word, his truth, come to us outside the words of the Bible? Absolutely. We hear God's truth expressed all the time, in many ways and places.

But would we be wise to neglect the sacraments and the

Bible just because God's grace and truth can operate outside these two vehicles? That would be foolish, presumptuous, and ungrateful. The sacraments are gifts from God, and it makes sense to understand and use them as he intends.

With this in mind, let's take a look at the very first gift in the whole sacramental order. This is baptism, the gateway to the whole Christian life.

Water That Purifies

You might wonder why God chose water as the sign of baptism. After all, God could have directed us to be baptized in vinegar. (Some Christians look as though they *have* been baptized in vinegar!) Many of us would have liked it if God had chosen wine. But as with all the sacramental signs, God chose water very carefully; its multiple meanings reveal so much about what it means to be a Christian.

First of all, water is cleansing, which is why Scripture sometimes refers to baptism as being washed (see Heb 10:22; Ti 3:5; Eph 5:26). Through the water of baptism we are purified from sin, as Peter told the crowd in his Pentecost sermon: "Repent, and be baptized every one of you in the name of Jesus Christ for the forgiveness of your sins" (Acts 2:38). This cleansing happens through what God did for us in Christ's death on the cross, not through our efforts to be good. Being plunged into the water of baptism is being washed in Christ's blood. We are saved by his grace, saved by what *he* has done (see Eph 2:8-9).

This is a truth that brings me hope whenever I start getting overwhelmed about being the halfhearted, lukewarm Christian that I often am. I remind myself that my salvation doesn't depend on what I do through my own power. What counts is what happened to me in my baptism, when Christ took me to himself and washed me in his own blood. So when I feel despondent, I remember my baptism. I remember that I am forgiven. I am clean!

Also, when I'm tempted to sin, I think about what it cost Christ to give me that white garment of baptism. "Do I really want to do this?" I ask myself. And the answer is clear. "No. I can't. It's not worth it. I don't want to soil the baptismal garment that Christ has given me."

Baptized Into Christ's Death

Water isn't just for cleansing. Its destructive power is awesome, as we see in the Old Testament. The Great Flood destroyed evil from the face of the earth so that God could begin things anew. In the Red Sea the Lord wiped out Pharaoh's forces and liberated Israel from slavery.

This is part of the meaning of the baptismal waters. Baptism doesn't just cleanse us; it makes us free! Before, we were in bondage to Satan. In baptism, we're liberated, set free to belong completely to Christ and be under his dominion.

Baptism destroys our old self, that is, the willful existence of running our own life independent of God. We come out of baptism as a new creation belonging to Christ and submitting ourselves to his will. "I have been crucified with Christ;" St. Paul says in Galatians 2:20; "it is no longer I who live, but Christ who lives in me." Elsewhere, he says that when we are baptized, we are baptized into Christ's death (see Rom 6:3-4). In other words, it's in baptism that our self-will is crucified with Christ. But this reality is something that must work itself out every day in Christian life. Living our baptism means saying yes to the Lord on a daily basis: "Your will and not mine."

By the age of sixteen, I had achieved a measure of success that seemed to point to a long-term, exciting career in rock music. As I came closer to the Lord, though, I heard him call me away from where I thought I wanted to go. In a troubling but unmistakable way, he made it clear that I was to lay down my bass guitar on the altar and prepare for a career in the church. I knew that this would take not just four years of college but at least four years of graduate school. The idea seemed absurd, especially given my aversion to study and terrible high school grades. But as I prayed and sought counsel, it seemed that this was indeed what God was saying to me. I said yes.

Amazingly, I got into college that year and found that I loved it! God had turned on in me the desire to learn about the world, about history and theology and so many other things. If I had pointed myself in the direction that *I* thought would lead to happiness, I would have been miserable. Surrendering to Christ, I discovered, is saying yes to a master who loves me more than I love myself, who knows me better than I know myself. What a dramatic contrast to Satan, that taskmaster who is out for our destruction!

Signed with the Cross

The ancient Romans had a ceremony that provides a good illustration of the kind of change of allegiance that baptism brings about. The *sacramentum* (from which our word "sacrament" comes) was a religious ceremony in which a soldier pledged lifelong obedience to the commander of his legion. Often his arm would be branded with the name of his commander or legion. In return for this pledge of service, the commander would swear to take care of the soldier for the rest of his life. The brand mark, then, was a sign not only of servitude but also of protection. Anyone who messed with the soldier would have to answer to his commander!

A similar sign of protection appears in the story of Cain and Abel. Cain kills his brother and is banned from human society and sentenced to wander the earth in exile. Then, because Cain is afraid that other people will kill him, the Lord puts a mark on him that means, "If you touch Cain, you deal with *me*" (see Gn 4:8-16). In the New Testament book of Revelation, it's Christ's faithful followers who get the protective sign. The four destroying angels are told: "Do not harm the earth or the sea or the trees, till we have sealed the servants of our God upon their foreheads" (Rv 7:3). They are sealed with the names of God and the Lamb (see Rv 14:1).

In baptism, our foreheads are marked with the sign of the cross. This protective seal identifies us as Christ's and warns Satan to get his hands off. It is also a pledge to accept Jesus Christ as our Lord and Savior. What the sign of the cross really means is this: "I belong no longer to myself but to the Father, Son, and Holy Spirit. My life is totally committed to God's will and purposes."

The sign of the cross, which comes from baptism, was probably used in New Testament times. Certainly, it was in use by the church no later than the second century. Around A.D. 215, St. Hippolytus gave Christians in Rome this advice: "When tempted, always reverently seal your forehead with the sign of the cross. For this sign of the passion is displayed and made manifest against the devil, if you make it in faith.... If indeed the adversary sees the power of the Spirit outwardly displayed in the image of baptism, he takes to flight trembling."

We should never make the sign of the cross in a mechanical, ritualistic manner. It has value, as Hippolytus says, when we make it in faith. Indeed, it is the sign of Christian faith, and when we make it, we are renewing our baptismal commitment to live for Christ alone. This is not a once-in-a-lifetime decision, but one that must be affirmed every day—even many times a day. That's why the sign of the cross is used so often in Catholic prayer and life.

Living Water, Life-Giving Power

Water doesn't just destroy and cleanse. It's also a sign of new life. Our natural, physical life begins in water, in our mother's womb, where we're carried for forty weeks. Our supernatural birth comes out of water as well. The baptismal font is like the womb of the church, who is our mother.

The connection between new birth and baptism comes out in Jesus' interchange with Nicodemus, the Pharisee who comes to Jesus for a night consultation (see Jn 3:1-21). Jesus tells him, "Truly, truly, I say to you, unless one is born anew, he cannot see the kingdom of God." Nicodemus doesn't get it. "How can a man be born when he is old? Can he enter a second time into his mother's womb and be born?" But no, that's not at all what Jesus means: "Truly, truly, I say to you, unless one is born of water and the Spirit, he cannot enter the kingdom of God" (Jn 3:3-5).

Unmistakably, Jesus is describing baptism. When our old life is put to death, the Lord gives us a brand-new life that comes because the Spirit comes. Later in John's Gospel, when Jesus speaks to the Samaritan woman at the well, Jesus actually talks about the Holy Spirit in terms of water. "Living water," he calls the Spirit—living water that becomes in believers a source that bubbles up and ensures they never thirst again (see Jn 4:10, 14).

Through this "living water" of baptism, we are given power to be new people. Baptism isn't a matter of dedicating ourselves to the Lord by living a hard, grinding life of sheer willpower. I tried that for a while and it didn't work. Without the power of the Spirit, it's easy to burn out. Just try putting the Sermon on the Mount into practice on your own, and you'll see what I mean. It's magnificent, but it's impossible to live out on human power alone.

What *bad* news the Good News would be if it were simply about impossible moral ideals! But the gospel *is* good news because the Lord doesn't just give commandments and ideals; he puts his very life within us and gives us power to be new people. That power of the Holy Spirit is what is communicated to us in baptism.

In this new life that comes through being "born of water and the Spirit," we become sons and daughters of God. To each of us personally he is "Abba"—not an overlord, judge, and taskmaster but our Father who loves us tenderly. There are many religions in the world and many people who believe in God, but no one ever spoke about God as Father the way Jesus did. Only Jesus has this kind of intimate relationship with God. Inviting us into his relationship with the Father is part of the beauty and magnificence of the gift Jesus offers us.

The Father's love is unconditional. It doesn't go away, and neither does the mark of the cross received in baptism. That mark is a sign of an inward mark on our soul. It signifies that we belong to the Father and are his children, no matter what we do. If we're prodigal sons and daughters, we may drift away from our Father, repudiate him, spit in his face. Still, like the prodigal son in Jesus' parable (see Lk 15:11-32), we remain sons and daughters. Wayward and full of weaknesses though we may be, we remain his children. How comforting to know that we're accepted and loved unconditionally and that if we return to our Father, we will always be welcomed back!

Being born into a relationship with God as Father means we are born into a family. It puts us in relationship with God's other sons and daughters and makes us members of the body of Christ, the church: "For by one Spirit we were all baptized into one body" (1 Cor 12:13).

Catholic teaching has always held that every baptized person, regardless of denomination, is joined in some marvelous way to the Catholic Church. We recognize all the baptized as brothers and sisters. There's a bond of unity that can't be taken away from us, despite the fact that our churches are still not fully united.

Let the Children Come

This sacrament of unity raises a question that has divided Christians over the past four hundred years: should infants be baptized? Catholics answer "yes," as do many other Christian denominations. But some Christians disagree. They reason that babies can't make the necessary kind of faith commitment. Babies can't understand the power of the Spirit and apply it in their lives.

Why, then, *do* Catholics baptize children and include them as members of the church? Why not just dedicate them to God or pray for them?

The fact that children are welcomed in the kingdom is demonstrated by what Jesus told the apostles who wanted to keep the children away from him. "Let the children come to me," he insisted, "do not hinder them; for to such belongs the kingdom of God" (Mk 10:14).

If you put this together with what Jesus said to Nicodemus—unless you be born of water and the Spirit, you can't enter the kingdom of God (see Jn 3:5)—it's clear that children ought to be welcomed into the kingdom through baptism, regardless of the fact that they can't yet speak for themselves. The first writers to mention infant baptism, in the third century, said that this practice was indeed taught to the church by the apostles.

But infant baptism isn't just a practice that's allowed by Scripture and taught by early tradition. It has a powerful meaning in itself. As the *Catechism of the Catholic Church* points out: "The sheer gratuitousness of the grace of salvation"—the fact that it's pure gift—"is particularly manifested in infant Baptism" (par. 1250).* We can't earn salvation—not even by an act of faith or by a decision. All we can do is accept it.

This is what children do: when they are baptized, they receive salvation as a pure gift. This underlines the reality that for *all* of us, it's a pure gift. Even for adults, any "yes" to God is always preceded and enabled by grace. Infant baptism highlights this truth, showing without a doubt that Catholics believe we are saved by grace not by works. "Our justification comes from the grace of God," says the *Catechism*. "Grace is *favor*, the *free and undeserved help* that God gives us to respond to his call to become children of God" (par. 1996).

Infant baptism also shows us that faith isn't an individualistic thing. It's not a solo flight, but a communal reality. The faith of the church gives rise to our faith. When we believe, we believe together with the whole body of believers. Faith is *caught* and not simply *taught*. That's why the church is a mother, giving birth to our faith just as the Holy Spirit gives birth to our relationship to God as Father. When infants are baptized, the faith of the Church stands in proxy for their own faith. Of course, as they grow, they must take responsibility to "own" and nourish the faith they received as a gift.

Unlocking the Spirit's Power

Now here's a big problem. Many people are baptized as children but don't have the slightest inkling of what baptism really means. This is how it was for me until age sixteen. Though I went to church and often made the sign of the cross, I didn't consciously regard Jesus as the Lord of my life. In fact, I was pretty convinced that doing good works—helping the poor and obeying the commandments—were what made me a Christian. Christ was a part of my life but certainly not the center of it. If anyone had told me that I needed to surrender control to him, I probably would have dismissed the idea as irresponsible! Not surprisingly, I didn't experience much of the power of the Spirit.

Or did I? Actually, once I entered into a more personal relationship with God and started reflecting on my life, I realized that I *had* been experiencing the Spirit's power all along. Because I was baptized as an infant, I went to church, heard God's word, and received the sacraments regularly as I was growing up. Sure, it didn't mean as much to me as it could and should have. (But then, it still doesn't ... I'm a work in progress!) And yet, there was some power in me that caused me to refrain from the destructive activity that nearly all my friends engaged in—drug use and even addiction, promiscuous sex with all its tragic side effects. I know now that this power was not me. It was the power of the Spirit received at baptism and nourished in the sacraments.

Not until I went through my personal Pentecost did the Spirit's full power begin to be unlocked in me. It happened as I went through a course of basic Christian teaching and learned what it really means that Jesus is Lord and Savior. At that point, the Holy Spirit began to move much more perceptibly in my life. Especially remarkable was the freedom I experienced from a pattern of sin that I had been unable to break. This freedom has lasted to this day.

On the other hand, there are faults and sins with which I continue to struggle. These too have been conquered in Christ, I know, but further work is needed for his victory to be complete in me. All of which goes to show that no matter when a Christian's spiritual awakening takes place, the work of conversion is never really done.

True conversion takes place through coming to know the Lord in an increasingly intimate way. This is why the Catholic Church constantly calls us to develop a personal relationship with Christ. Lacking this, a person will tend to receive the sacraments somewhat mechanically, as I used to, and to live a life that has some religious externals but isn't fully given over to God.

John Paul II pinpointed this problem a few years ago in a homily that was reprinted in the Vatican newspaper. He observed that often Catholics have never had the chance to experience Jesus Christ personally as the way, the truth, and the life (see *L'Osservatore Romano,* English ed., March 24, 1993, 3). In another homily, the pope told a group of German bishops interested in evangelization that "only from a personal relationship with Jesus can an effective evangelization develop" (see *L'Osservatore Romano,* English ed., Dec. 23-30, 1992, 5-6).

Accepting Jesus Christ as our personal Lord and Savior, which is basically what the pope has been saying we need to do, isn't just a onetime deal. Every single day we're called to throw off our old self more and more and plunge deeper into Christ. It's a lifetime project, as the Holy Father brings out in this passage from his encyclical, "The Mission of the Redeemer" (par. 46):

> From the outset, conversion is expressed in faith which is total and radical, and which neither limits nor hinders God's gift. At the same time, it gives rise to a dynamic and lifelong process which demands a continual turning away from "life according to the flesh" to "life according to the Spirit" (cf. Rom 8:3-13). Conversion means accepting, by a personal decision, the saving sovereignty of Christ and becoming his disciple.

Remember Your Baptism

One aid to ongoing conversion is to remember our baptism and what it means. Though most of us aren't aware of it, the Catholic Church provides just such a reminder in its life every week. This is Sunday Mass, which is, among other things, a renewal of baptism. Consider these elements:

—*Holy water.* Dipping our fingers into the holy water font and blessing ourselves on the way into church is a renewal of our baptism. It signifies that only through baptism do we have the right to enter God's house and be called his sons and daughters. Only because we are baptized can we go forward to the altar, to the family table, the table of Christ.

—*The Sign of the Cross.* From a small mark traced on the forehead of the person being baptized, the sign of the cross which begins every Mass has become a larger gesture that covers the whole top half of the body. St. Hippolytus said that this sign is a shield. Like soldiers using their shields to cover as much of themselves as possible, we make the sign of the cross to ask the Lord's protection. We rededicate ourselves to the service of Jesus Christ and we repudiate the enemy. Every time we make this sign, we announce that we're going to live as Christ's disciples.

—*The Creed.* At Sunday Mass we say the Creed. This profession of faith grew out of the baptismal liturgy. Originally it consisted of three simple questions, each one followed by the affirmation, "I do": "Do you accept God the Father Almighty, Creator of heaven and earth?... Jesus Christ, his only Son our Lord?... Do you believe in the Holy Spirit?" With its three "I dos," baptism is a wedding ceremony, and we repeat those pledges in expanded form every time we recite the Creed at Sunday Mass.

—*Receiving Communion.* When we come forward to receive the body and blood of Christ, we leave our old life on the altar. It's an opportunity to decide once again that we will live for Christ, setting aside our own life to take on his.

The sacrament of penance is also a renewal of baptism. We can be baptized in water, sacramentally, just once. But we can be baptized again and again in the mercy of God in the sacrament of penance.

In addition to these reminders of baptism, many Catholics recall the event and its significance by celebrating their baptismal birthdays. That's what we do in my family. You might want to consider doing the same. Find out what days you and others in your family were baptized and celebrate these for what they are: the most important days of your lives! Take the celebration as an opportunity to renew your baptismal vows. Do it together with your family, if your family is Christian. Do it alone, if need be. But don't let your spiritual birthday go by uncelebrated.

And Finally...

A word to readers who have fallen in love with Christ—maybe through something like the personal Pentecost I had in my teens—but are wondering what this experience has to do with sacramental baptism.

For those of you who have been baptized already, know that there is a connection between the two events. Your new Pentecost is a release, a bringing into experience of something that was given you a long time ago but sat in the deep freeze. It's been thawed out and activated. There is no need to be baptized again. What *is* necessary is that you commit yourself to God and renew the power of baptism on a daily basis.

For those of you who haven't yet been baptized, know that baptism isn't something superfluous. It's not an afterthought. It really is a gift of God that will communicate more power and life that will bind you to the Father and to the church in a new and deeper way.

For all of us, let's examine ourselves to see how much we really appreciate our baptism. Do we know what it means? Do we take pride in the great gift we've been given?

A priest friend of mine—a great preacher and scholar who holds a doctorate in theology—has only one thing hanging on the wall in his office. It's not any of his many academic degrees or awards. It's his baptismal certificate. That's the importance of baptism in his life. That's the importance it ought to hold in ours.

Chapter Three

Confirmation: Empowered to Serve

All Christians baptize, but only a few denominations see the need of an anointing following baptism called confirmation. Why does the Catholic Church insist that this sacramental anointing is important? Isn't it enough to have been washed clean, made God's sons and daughters, and filled with the Holy Spirit in baptism?

To answer this question, let's look at the New Testament, the ultimate norm of our faith and the place where teaching on the sacraments always begins.

Pentecost Experiences in Scripture

Jesus is the model of what happens to the Christian. All four Gospels speak of his baptism by John in the Jordan. When Jesus emerges from the water, the Holy Spirit descends on him in the visible form of a dove, and the Father cries out, "This is my beloved Son, in whom I am well pleased" (see Mk 1:9-11).

Immediately, Jesus' life changes. This carpenter who had lived a quiet life with his mother is now led out by the Spirit into the desert. For forty days he battles Satan through prayer and fasting. Then he comes back, enters the synagogue of Nazareth, takes up a scroll, and proclaims the first two verses of Isaiah 61. You can imagine the townspeople's surprise when this ordinary craftsman reads this:

> "The Spirit of the Lord is upon me,
> because he has anointed me to preach good news to the poor.
> He has sent me to proclaim release to the captives
> and recovering of sight to the blind,
> to set at liberty those who are oppressed,
> to proclaim the acceptable year of the Lord."
>
> LUKE 4:18-19

This describes what happened to Jesus after baptism, when the Spirit anointed him to fight and to serve. Immediately Jesus began working miracles, teaching the crowds, healing the sick, and driving out demons. For three years the kingdom of God was evident in his dynamic ministry.

The same thing later happened to his disciples. Though they had followed Jesus for three years, witnessed his miracles, and even seen his risen body, they were still very reserved about their faith. Fifty days after the first Easter, they were even praying behind closed doors for fear of the authorities! The Pentecostal fire that fell upon them that day (see Acts 2) was the same anointing that Jesus had received in the Jordan. It empowered the disciples to work the same miracles as were worked by Christ.

Some Christians who were not in the upper room on the day of Pentecost received a similar outpouring of the Spirit. Certain Samaritan Christians "received the Holy Spirit" (Acts 8:17) after Peter and John came and laid their hands on them. And Paul found some Christians in Ephesus who had not even heard of the Holy Spirit. He baptized them in the name of Jesus; then he laid hands on them, and the Spirit came in a dramatic way (see Acts 19:1-7).

What the New Testament shows, then, is that the Spirit normally is poured out on a Christian after baptism through the laying on of hands of an apostle. That's really what confirmation is all about: the coming of the Spirit through the intercession of the bishop, a successor of the apostles.

What's in a Name?

Essentially, confirmation gives us a share in Jesus' anointing for service. The name "Christ" means "anointed one"; it points to Jesus' empowerment by the Spirit to liberate, serve, and save. When Jesus calls us to follow him, he doesn't mean for us to make our way to heaven alone; we're called to bring others with us. We can only do this through a special share in his anointing. This is why, early on, Jesus' followers came to be known as Christians, "anointed ones."

We're so used to this name that it doesn't strike us as especially meaningful. But for awhile in the early church, Jesus' followers were also called "Nazarenes" and "followers of The Way." They were called Christians for the first time in Antioch (see Acts 11:26), the city from which Paul was sent out on the journeys that brought the gospel to the whole Greco-Roman world. It's no coincidence that the name "Christian" arose in a place so connected with missionary activity. It highlights the fact that to be a follower of Jesus means to share in his mission. This is a privilege that is not an option. It's a mandate and responsibility of everyone who goes by the name Christian, "anointed one."

Anointing is a practice with very ancient roots. In the Old Testament, it was done with a special olive oil that we call chrism. Now, I'm Italian, and I get excited about olive oil. But chrism wasn't just any old olive oil; it was oil perfumed with precious spices (see Ex 30:22-33). Chrism was so special that only priests, prophets, and kings were anointed with it.

The chrism used in confirmation is a perfumed oil blessed by the bishop. It recalls Jesus' anointing "with the Holy Spirit and with power" just after his baptism (Acts 10:38)—his threefold anointing as priest, king, and prophet. Through confirmation we become sharers in Jesus' priesthood, prophetic ministry, and kingly dignity.

The Tasks of a Priestly People

Psalm 133 talks about the "precious oil"—that wonderful chrism—flowing down on Aaron's beard. To us it sounds like a big laundry problem, but in the Old Testament this oil was a sign of abundance and joy. Since priests were consecrated with it, the chrism symbolized the rich gift of the Spirit upon the priesthood.

Christ is the great high priest who is prefigured in the Old Testament priesthood. To him first of all belongs the priestly anointing with the magnificent oil of the Holy Spirit. But amazingly, Christ shares this with us! Our anointing in confirmation calls us to share in Christ's priestly duty. (It also indicates that the Catholic Church has always believed in the priesthood of all believers.)

What's a priestly duty, anyway? In the Old Testament, priests offered sacrifice and interceded for the people. Christ did this too, though not by presenting animal sacrifices. Rather, he offered *himself* as a living sacrifice—a bloody, once-and-for-all sacrifice on the altar of the cross.

Likewise, our anointing as members of a priestly people (see 1 Pt 2:5, 9) calls us to offer ourselves to God. As Romans 12:1 puts it: "Present your bodies as a living sacrifice, holy and acceptable to God, which is your spiritual worship." This total self-offering is our vocation and privileged mission. The gospel is a free gift and so is salvation, but these free gifts cost us everything! All that we are and do must be offered to the Father as a pleasing sacrifice with Christ for the salvation of the world.

In my family, we take this as a daily task. Around the breakfast table, we offer our day as a sacrifice to God. Before I begin the day's work, I present it as a living sacrifice and ask the Lord to make it pleasing to him. This morning offering, which is part of the Catholic Tradition, is an exercise of the priesthood conferred on us in baptism and confirmation. It helps us to realize our particular call as lay people, which is to get into the nitty-gritty of human life—family, work, and everything else secular—so that it can be redeemed and sanctified. As God's priestly people make this offering day after day, all things are elevated and supernaturalized, transformed by the magnificent grace of Christ.

Another reason Christ is called high priest is because he intercedes. Even now, says the letter to the Hebrews, "he always lives to make intercession" for us (Heb 7:25). Through confirmation, we too are called to be intercessors, people who are in constant prayer not only for those we know and love but for the entire world. That's what the "Prayer of the Faithful" in the Mass is all about. There we remember the bigger picture. We pray for persecuted Christians, for church and government leaders, for the poor and the sick. This is part of the mission we're appointed to when we're confirmed. Of course our intercession is not to be limited to Mass; we're called to "pray constantly" (1 Thes 5:16) for the needs of all.

Foot-Washing: Kings Do It

Confirmation gives us a share in the Lord's kingly anointing. We have to remember, though, what kind of kingship our Messiah exercised.

Jesus was the kind of king who processed into Jerusalem on a donkey and whose only crown was made of thorns. While he manifested his power by binding the "strong man," Satan, Jesus demonstrated his dignity through his awesome humility. The night before he died, Jesus gave the most dramatic demonstration of this by kneeling to wash his disciples' feet (see Jn 13). In first-century Palestine, this was the most despicable job imaginable. Not even Israelite slaves could be commanded to perform it. By choosing this lowliest of tasks, Jesus showed us what his kind of kingship calls us to do for others.

The need for foot-washing isn't what it was in the days when people wore sandals and walked on dusty roads. In our society, the equivalent of this despised job might be changing a messy diaper—a task I'm very familiar with! But it isn't just parents who get to be modern-day foot-washers. Many people are called to the noble work of caring for the bodily needs of children, the elderly, the sick.

In one way or another, every follower of Christ is called to humble service. Strengthened by the kingly anointing received in confirmation, everyone can embrace that call.

This is true even for invalids and others who don't *look* like they're in much of a position to offer help. The humble kingship of Jesus' followers is often exercised in a hidden yet very powerful way. St. Thérèse of Lisieux lived behind monastery doors and so couldn't be the kind of missionary St. Paul was. But because she expressed her evangelistic zeal through the hidden work of intercession, Catholics honor her as patroness of the missions.

Through this humble, quiet gift of self, we can overthrow the power of the enemy. This is why Catholics seek Mary's prayers and turn to her as our most powerful intercessor against the forces of darkness. But in her lifetime Jesus' mother never did anything flashy. No exorcisms! No miracles! All she did was say her lowly, hidden "yes" to God's will—the most powerful weapon imaginable against Satan.

So many of us want to get out there and DO something once we experience our baptism and confirmation getting activated. I know I did when I was sixteen. I wanted to LEAD, to PREACH. Instead, my first job was to set up chairs in the church hall.

That was a great start. It helped me understand that sharing in the kingly mission of the Lord means joining an army of foot-washers. While our society teaches us to race to the top, in Christ's kingdom the race is to the bottom.

Who Speaks for God?

Finally, Jesus' anointing marks him out as a prophet greater than all the rest, including Elijah, Elisha, and Moses. Through his miracles, conversations, and entire being, Jesus was God's spokesman. This is a prophet's main job description. In fact, it's the literal meaning of the Greek word for prophet: one who speaks on behalf of another. Being a prophet has nothing necessarily to do with foretelling the future. To share in Jesus' prophetic anointing means being called to speak for the living God in our deeds and words—that is, to proclaim the gospel to all people.

When I was growing up, I thought only bishops and missionaries were called to evangelize. Looking around, I saw no need for spreading the gospel. "This is a Christian country," I reasoned. "No one here needs to be evangelized. That's for pagans in far-off lands."

Certainly, the work of foreign missions is an urgent necessity for the whole church. Ever since the Second Vatican Council, however, the church has been pointing to the emergence of a *new* evangelization, a work which every one of its members is called to embrace.

What's "new" about this evangelization? First of all, the mission field: our formerly Christian countries and societies must be reevangelized. A recent Gallup poll showed that the overwhelming majority of American churchgoers live in a way that is indistinguishable from the typical American way of life. Also, many people in our society are unchurched; they have no religious identity whatsoever and are hungering for meaning in their life. Who is going to speak for God to all these people? No way that missionaries, bishops, and religious alone can do the job. It's too big.

That's another reason this evangelization is called *new:* it needs to be carried out by new evangelizers. By people who may never have thought of themselves as missionaries. People like you and me.

Fortunately, confirmation equips *everybody* to proclaim the gospel. It "gives us a special strength of the Holy Spirit to spread and defend the faith by word and action as true witnesses of Christ" (*Catechism of the Catholic Church,* par. 1303). In fact, a Vatican II document pointed out that Catholics who have been confirmed are "more strictly obliged to spread the faith by word and deed" (*Lumen gentium,* par. 11).

I've heard a lot of homilies that advise, "Don't worry about talking about your faith. Just be a good example." But this is *not* the teaching of the church! Certainly, it's disgraceful to speak God's word without bearing witness to it by our actions. But a silent witness through example only is bad evangelizing too. If you never explain why your life is different—why you have a smile on your face and peace in your heart—people are likely to draw the wrong conclusions. Instead of seeing God in your life, they'll look at you and think, "Well, they're just well-adjusted folks. They have their act together. They've got gifts I don't."

I'm reminded of my own inability to share the gospel in those early days after I came to living faith in Christ. Some of my rock and roll friends noticed changes in my life and asked about them. These were great openings to talk about God, but I didn't know how.

"You're going to all these masses and classes and prayer meetings," my friends would observe. "You're different. What's going on?"

"Well, um ... I'm kind of learning ... um ... you know ... um ... that ... um ... there's more important things than money and sex ... and um ... and I need to help people."

"So you're into social work?"

"No. I'm ... I'm a ... I'm a Christian...." And that was about as far as my explanation could go.

I quickly realized that in order to explain my faith successfully, I needed to study it. Studying, understanding, and then speaking out boldly for God—this is part of what it means to share in Christ's prophetic anointing. The church is essentially missionary, so unless we accept the call to mission, we're not fully Catholic.

Confirmed, Commissioned, Empowered

If baptism is like getting your foot in the church door, confirmation is like coming into the hallway. There we are personally welcomed by the host of the house, the bishop, who is a successor of the apostles and the visible center of the local church. He is the original minister of confirmation who signs and seals those receiving the sacrament.

The connection with the apostles is also evoked when confirmation is conferred by a priest, since the sacred chrism he uses must be blessed by the bishop. Whether present in person or through the use of this blessed oil, the bishop is our living link with those to whom Jesus first entrusted the great commission to "go into all the world and preach the gospel to the whole creation" (Mk 16:15). In confirmation he conveys that commission to others.

Fortunately, the Lord never imposes obligations without equipping us to carry them out. As we're anointed, we're empowered to serve as apostles, evangelists, intercessors, servants. Because God's word never returns to him empty, things happen through the sacramental signs and words of confirmation. The Holy Spirit, a Spirit of power, is always given to us. We can count on it.

The prophet Isaiah describes the Spirit and his power in terms of seven gifts that rest upon the Messiah: wisdom, understanding, counsel, fortitude, knowledge, piety, and fear of the Lord (see Is 11:2). Poured out on Jesus as the anointed king, this sevenfold Spirit is likewise poured out on us in confirmation.

Each of these gifts is fabulous and would warrant a book in itself. Here are reflections on just four of them.

Fortitude. This supernatural courage characterizes the apostles once the Spirit comes at Pentecost. What a transformation! Fearful no more, they burst out into the same streets through which Jesus was dragged to Calvary, proclaiming publicly that Jesus is risen from the dead. Their bold witnessing has a powerful effect: "about three thousand souls" are baptized and added to the church that day (Acts 2:41).

Stories like this comfort me. Even though I'm not courageous by nature, I know that the Holy Spirit can give me *supernatural* courage when I need it. All I have to do is yield to this gift of holy boldness.

Counsel. Though I've done my best to educate my mind, it remains woefully inadequate. I have very limited information, especially when it comes to major life decisions. "Should I get married? Who would I marry? Join a religious order? Which one?" When it comes to such awesome issues, you can't just decide by making a list of pros and cons. God knows that, which is why he grants us a gift of supernatural guidance, subtly prompting and attracting us to the way he wants us to go.

It's kind of scary to make decisions this way, relying on supernatural guidance along with what we can reason out. Something in us would like the process to be purely rational. But a toggle sheet is no guarantee against mistakes. Instead, the Lord calls us to unpack the gift of counsel and learn to use it. Guidance from more experienced Christians can be a great help in this. Still, it's important to know that the wonderful gift of supernatural guidance is available to every baptized and confirmed Christian.

Understanding. Through the power of the Spirit, we're equipped to understand biblical truths with our heart, not just our rational mind. The Holy Spirit helps us to penetrate their meaning in a supernatural way. This is how St. Thomas Aquinas explains the spiritual gift of understanding.

This certainly rings true to my own experience. Following my personal Pentecost, I developed a hunger for the Bible. Things I had found boring and meaningless suddenly came to life; they nourished and excited me. If this has happened to you, too, know that this is the gift of understanding. If this gift hasn't been activated in you yet, ask the Holy Spirit's help. The gift is already yours through confirmation.

Piety. As a teenager walking into the first session of a "basic Christianity" course, I was surprised by the wide variety of people attending. They came from different ethnic and racial groups, from both sides of the generation gap. Some were in business suits, others were long-hairs like me. Coming during a time of political polarization in the U.S., a gathering like this astounded me.

Even more astonishing were the deep relationships that developed among us. These began when, through the gift of piety, the Holy Spirit gave us all affection for God as Father—not just fear of him as Lord and Master. This led us to recognize each other as brothers and sisters, children of the same Father. Though we had little in common on the natural level, we experienced a bond of love that went way beyond anything we could have expected.

No matter what external differences separate us, we Christians have a common life as God's family that leads to mutual affection. This happens through the Spirit's gift of piety, received in confirmation.

"Accept the Charisms With Gratitude!"

The Holy Spirit also brings us gifts called "charisms." While the "seven gifts of the Spirit" build us up and enable us to grow in sanctity, charisms enable us to build up the church and serve others. Charisms are supernatural gifts of grace, but sometimes they build on humble, natural foundations. That's the way God usually works: grace builds on nature; it perfects and elevates it.

Having always believed in and encouraged charisms, the Catholic Church is officially charismatic. It's the largest Pentecostal church in the world! The *Catechism* calls the charisms a "wonderfully rich grace for the apostolic vitality and for the holiness of the entire Body of Christ" (see *Catechism*, pars. 799-801). The Second Vatican Council, in its "Dogmatic Constitution on the Church," teaches that the Holy Spirit "distributes special graces among the faithful of every rank.... These charismatic gifts, whether they be the most outstanding or the more simple and widely diffused, are to be received with thanksgiving and consolation, for they are exceedingly suitable and useful for the needs of the church" (*Lumen gentium,* par. 12).

More dramatically, on Pentecost 1998, John Paul II said: "Today to all of you, and to all Christians, I want to cry out: Be open and docile to the gifts of the Holy Spirit. Accept with gratitude and obedience the charisms that the Spirit never ceases to bestow. Come, Holy Spirit, and make the charisms you have bestowed ever more fruitful."

What charisms does the Spirit bring? I can't enumerate them, because charisms are so varied, numerous, and specific to particular needs that they can't be compiled into an exhaustive list. One famous listing in 1 Corinthians 12 mentions charisms like *teaching*: supernatural instruction that gives inspiration as well as information. There's the mountain-moving *faith* that Jesus talks about in the Gospels. There's supernatural *healing* and *miracles, prophecy, discernment of spirits, tongues* and *interpretation of tongues.*

But 1 Corinthians 12 also speaks of humbler charisms. *Administration*, for example. Doesn't this sound like a gift for an accountant? Well, the charism of administration is broader than the ability to manage finances or business affairs. It refers to the Spirit-inspired ability to oversee a project, mission, or other service to God's people in a way that builds up the church, glorifies God, and doesn't bog down in bureaucracy.

Other humble charisms are mentioned in Romans 12. The ministry of *service* sounds unexciting—but remember, this is what Christ demonstrates in the footwashing episode of John 13. Housework for an elderly person, planning a Holy Week liturgy, working on a parish hospitality team—all these ordinary services are supernatural, if done with the joy and love of the Spirit.

Romans 12 also mentions the charism of *exhortation,* the ability to motivate others to greater love and service of Christ. Calling people on without cajoling and browbeating, in a way that inspires, uplifts, and encourages is a supernatural gift. Doing *works of mercy* is a charism (see Rom 12:8). Some so-called charitable works demean people, keep them dependent, and take away their dignity. What a contrast with the way Mother Teresa and her sisters would perform these works! One with those they serve, they enhance and elevate the dignity of the poorest of the poor and make them feel like the princes and princesses they really are in God's eyes.

Another mention of charisms appears in 1 Corinthians 7:7, where Paul calls *Christian marriage* itself a charism. Marriage is a natural institution which offers many natural goods, such as companionship and children. A Christian marriage, though, is supernatural. Building on a natural foundation, it turns a marriage heavenward and bases it on the rock that is Christ. Christian marriage also reveals the love and unbreakable bond between Christ and his church.

Celibacy, too, is a charism of the Spirit, says St. Paul in the very same verse. He's not talking about people who stay single to have a fun-filled life without the burden of caring for children. Charismatic celibacy means being single in imitation of Christ, for the sake of greater freedom to serve a bigger family. It's a gift of love to the Lord and to the whole church.

Unwrapping Our Charismatic Gifts

Three points about the charisms. First, it's important to remember that they're *gifts* for the good of the church. We can't just pick out the ones we want and then use them on our own initiative. Our charisms need to be discerned and coordinated. Bishops, priests, and deacons have a special charism, received through ordination, for this discernment, and we should all work together with them to build up the whole church (see *Catechism,* par. 801).

Second, keep in mind that the humble charisms are just as important as the flashier ones. Now, I admit that I'd love to be able to raise the dead and work miracles! But this doesn't seem to be how God normally works through me. Right from the beginning, God called me to serve him in more ordinary ways—like offering my music as a gift for use in prayer and the liturgy. I saw my natural gift gradually transformed into a supernatural one that enables people to lift their hearts and minds to God.

If we're faithful in little things like this, the Lord will often give us greater gifts. Sometimes, the greater gifts are given right off the bat. There are people who prophesy and work miracles soon after their conversion. If this isn't our experience, though, we need to begin gratefully with what God has given us and be good stewards.

Finally, St. Paul gives us the most important directive of all about the Spirit's gifts when he teaches the preeminence of love. If I have spectacular gifts of tongues, prophecy, or healing but "have not love, I am nothing," he says (1 Cor 13:2). Every charism in the Christian life is intended to build and serve charity, or *agape*. This is the totally self-giving kind of love that God has for us and invites us to return to him and others. Without charity, everything is in vain (see *Catechism*, par. 800).

A Word to the Confirmed and the Not-Yet Confirmed

If you're awaiting confirmation or preparing others for this sacrament, I encourage you to realize that the *experience* of the Holy Spirit—his joy, gifts, and charisms—should be seen as normal for adults who are being confirmed. It destroys faith to entertain thoughts like, "Gee, this might not happen. Better not get my hopes up." The Holy Spirit does come in power, and we need to be prepared for that—disposed and ready to respond.

Interestingly, in the early church receiving the Spirit seemed to be a perceptible experience; it made a difference that was noticeable to everyone. Otherwise, how could Paul have asked the Galatians: "Did you experience so many things in vain...? Does, then, the one who supplies the Spirit to you and works mighty deeds among you do so from works of the law or from faith in what you heard?" (Gal 3:4-5, NAB).

This palpable coming of the Spirit was also reported by Church Fathers writing over an eight-hundred-year period in both the East and the West. As shown in a 1991 study by two accomplished theologians, biblical scholar George Montague and patristics scholar Kilian McDonnell, the Fathers indicated that adults who were baptized and confirmed *experienced* a difference in their lives. In the words of St. Hilary of Poitiers, "We who have been reborn through the sacrament of baptism experience intense joy when we feel within us the first stirrings of the Holy Spirit." Speaking of the charisms right afterwards, he adds,

"Let us make use of such generous gifts." (See *Fanning the Flame*, Collegeville, Minn.: Liturgical Press, 1991, 16.)

"But I've already been confirmed," some people say, "and I didn't feel anything happening."

This is certain: the grace and power of the Spirit really were communicated to you in confirmation. But the gifts need to be unpacked. It's like getting a new credit card that can't be used until you call and get it activated. St. Paul uses another image to make the same point when he tells Timothy to "stir into flame the gift of God that you have through the imposition of my hands" (2 Tm 1:6, NAB).

There are sparks deep within everyone who has been confirmed. Some of us have already felt them leaping up into the fire of the Holy Spirit. Others need to pray that the sparks will burst into flame and that the gifts of the Spirit will be activated and become fruitful for the life of the church.

It's easy to shrink back at the prospect of exercising these spiritual gifts. "I need more preparation, more prayer, more study," we tell the Lord. But let's put fear and procrastination aside. God has given us charisms because the world urgently needs to hear the good news. People are desperate for it. And if we don't share it with them, we'll be held responsible.

"What have I done with my baptism? How do I answer my vocation? What have I done with my confirmation? Have I used the gifts and charisms of the Spirit to bear fruit?" These are the fundamental questions that Pope John Paul II suggests we ask ourselves in light of this new millennium. For each of us, may these questions serve as both an examination of conscience and a spur to action. Let's ask for the strength of the Spirit to respond to God's call and live out the grace of confirmation.

Chapter Four

Personal Prayer: Pathway to Joy

I've never met anyone who doesn't want to be happy. People are different in many ways, but the search for joy and happiness is common to us all.

But where is this happiness to be found? Judging from what you hear on the radio, most people believe that joy comes from love. In Texas, where I live, country music is king. Nearly every country song is about love, and their titles often make me grin: "I've Flushed You from the Toilet of My Heart" ... "If You Don't Leave Me Alone, I'll Go and Find Someone Else Who Will" ... "She Made Toothpicks out of the Timber of My Heart." They're humorous—and yet, I think they're onto something.

It's only in an intimate relationship that human beings are fulfilled and able to find happiness. Such love is what we were created for. The problem is that many assume that only *romantic* love can satisfy us. Of course, a romantic love is a great gift from God—and even greater than we can realize. The letter to the Ephesians speaks of the intimate union of man and woman as a profound "mystery" (the word can also be translated "sacrament") and a sign pointing beyond itself to an awesome, supernatural reality: it refers to Christ and the church (see Eph 5:22).

Wonderful as it is, marriage, with its romantic love, can't begin to compare with the union between Christ and his church. Into this union, each member of Christ is invited. All of us—whether single, married, divorced, or widowed—can have this intimate relationship with Christ that makes for true joy and happiness.

The Ways of Prayer

How is this intimate relationship with the Lord developed? Catholic teaching stresses the centrality of prayer and, in particular, of the Eucharist. What could be more conducive to knowing and loving Jesus than receiving his body and blood, soul and divinity—his very self—under the forms of bread and wine? Because it's our most personal and intimate contact with God, the Eucharist is called the source and summit of the whole Christian life.

But just as every mountaintop needs a mountain to sit on, the Eucharist is intended to crown a life of prayer and intimacy with God. It isn't meant to stand alone. A precious gem needs a setting or it will fall off the ring and be lost. Similarly, a beautiful painting needs a frame to set it off and bring it into perspective. Again, that's what a life of prayer is all about. It provides the proper setting for the Eucharist, lest the grace of the sacrament be lost. Prayer is a living context that surrounds the Eucharist and helps it bear maximum fruit in our lives.

We'll discuss the Eucharist in chapters five and six and focus here on the regular, personal dialogue with God that forms its context day by day. First, a few general comments about some of the many types of prayer.

The Lord encourages us to use a myriad of approaches to prayer. In fact, I like to think of our need for different kinds of prayer as resembling our need for a balanced diet.

Small group prayer is one of the items in this spiritual diet. "Where two or three are gathered in my name, there am I in the midst of them," Jesus promised (Mt 18:20). The *Catechism of the Catholic Church* identifies prayer groups as "one of the signs and one of the driving forces of renewal of prayer in the church...." (par. 2689). Sometimes groups pray the rosary or the psalms, hymns, and prayers of the Divine Office, or other formal prayers.

It's also great to get together and pray informally by offering extemporaneous prayers of praise and intercession. Now, I realize that most Catholics aren't used to praying out loud spontaneously. I certainly wasn't. The first time I prayed aloud in a group, I was so embarrassed I could barely whisper, "Praise you, Jesus ... (cough, cough).... I love you, ... (cough) ... God." My father, a church-going Catholic, was so inhibited that for thirty years he couldn't even bring himself to recite a formal prayer with the family. Not until he was in his sixties and came into a deeper, living relationship with the Lord did this change.

Even if you feel inhibited about informal vocal prayer, give it a try anyway. It gets easier—even enjoyable!

Besides praying in groups, we can pray throughout the day by talking to the Lord. If you've seen the musical "Fiddler on the Roof," you'll remember that this is what characterizes the main character, Tevye. I love this story and its portrayal of this Jewish man in constant, honest conversation with God—thanking, complaining, asking for help as he goes about his daily business. It reminds me of what the great fourth-century

Church Father, John Chrysostom, set forth as an ideal for us Christians: "It's possible to offer fervent prayer even while walking in public or strolling alone, or seated in your shop,... while buying or selling,... or even while cooking."

Personal Prayer: Practical Ins and Outs

However much we need the Eucharist, along with the other items that make up a balanced prayer diet, there's no substitute for dedicated quiet time alone with the Lord. It's like any other relationship. For example, a husband and wife are together a lot in daily tasks like cooking, shopping, and taking care of the kids. They also need quality time as a couple, where they can give each other undivided attention. So, too, in our relationship with our heavenly spouse, the Lord Jesus. We must spend one-on-one time with him on a regular basis.

Jesus told us to gather together for the Eucharist: "Do this in remembrance of me" (Lk 22:19). He encouraged us to pray in small groups (Mt 18:20). But Jesus also directed his followers to turn to God in private prayer: "When you pray," he said, "go into your room and shut the door and pray to your Father who is in secret" (Mt 6:6).

Jesus expects us to develop a life of regular personal prayer, and so this has been an important part of Catholic life from the beginning. This makes sense, because prayer is nourishment. Would you go a day without eating? No matter how busy we are, we all make time to eat. Well, prayer is our daily bread. To hear God's word and talk with him regularly is nourishment our souls can't live without.

If you've already tried to establish a routine of personal prayer, you know that the first step involves confronting some hard scheduling issues. *When shall I pray? How long shall I pray?* The answers to these questions will probably vary from one season of life to another. This I know from my own experience.

Like many Christians over the centuries, I was moved by Jesus' invitation to three of his disciples to "watch one hour" with him in the Garden of Gethsemane (Mk 14:37). They fell asleep on the job, and when I first tried spending an hour with the Lord I wasn't so successful either. But I worked up to it over a few months, and for awhile I had a great prayer life. I was single at the time and found it easy to set aside an hour for daily personal prayer plus daily Mass. I also prayed together with friends from time to time. Even after I got married, this arrangement was workable, and Susan and I prayed together daily.

Then our twins were born, and my schedule was totally shot. I loved those babies but they were a couple of rascals! They didn't like to sleep—especially not at the same time. Every morning at five they needed a bottle-feeding, which was my responsibility. For the first nine months after their birth, Susan and I were blithering idiots, walking around sleep-deprived and semiconscious. Consequently, my hour or more of daily personal prayer came to a sudden end. The most I could do was to stave off sleep by dragging myself around the block and praying one decade of the rosary after that five a.m. feeding. This was the pattern that sustained my relationship with the Lord on a daily basis for close to a year. Unsatisfactory as it seemed, this period became for me a time of tremendous grace and character growth.

What this experience taught me is that God honors our

efforts to do what we can to spend time with him. We simply need to start somewhere, depending on our state in life and other circumstances.

Probably most of us can find at least fifteen or twenty minutes in which to give the Lord our undivided attention. What time of day will work best? For many people, it's first thing in the morning. This was true for me when I started my prayer life. Because my days were filled with busyness, I got into the pattern of praying before anyone else got up. Then, because I found myself falling asleep, I decided to preface my prayer time with a bit of exercise. My whole athletic life began as an effort to be awake for prayer!

As even early mornings became busy, I switched to other tactics. For a while I tried staying up late and praying after everyone else went to bed and the phone stopped ringing. Unfortunately, I usually fell asleep. My current solution is to pray in the middle of the day. Instead of taking a whole hour for lunch, I go to a nearby chapel and spend time before the Blessed Sacrament. Sometimes I pray outdoors; worries and distractions melt away as I contemplate God's creation and lift up my heart to him.

Finding time to pray sometimes requires creativity. I just heard about a mother of small children who, after many failed attempts to establish a regular time for prayer, finally struck a deal with the Lord. Every day she tells him, "Whenever my first time of quiet comes up today, I won't read the paper or turn on the TV or make a phone call. For however long it lasts, I'll spend that time with you."

If you love the Lord enough and are determined to grow in him, you'll find a way to turn to him in daily prayer. If you don't see a solution, pray for one. With God assisting, something will work out.

Take Up, Read, and Listen!

Once people make time to pray, they often have trouble with prayer itself. Viewing prayer as a monologue—"I talk to God," or even "I need to tell God how I think things ought to be"—is probably the most common reason for this problem. But prayer is a *dialogue*. Furthermore, what's really important about it is what *God* says to us. God is the senior partner in this relationship, and we need to listen to him. Why do you suppose God gave us two ears and only one mouth? I think it's to show us that, in prayer, we should listen twice as much as we talk!

How *do* we listen to God in our personal prayer time? By pondering his written word. In Scripture, God has given us a regular opportunity to hear him speak a personal word that will nourish us and change our lives.

Although regular Bible reading is not a habit for most Catholics, the church calls us to read Scripture as much as we can. The Second Vatican Council was especially insistent on this point, stating that the church "forcefully and specifically exhorts all the Christian faithful ... to learn 'the surpassing knowledge of Jesus Christ' (Phil 3:8) by frequent reading of the divine Scriptures" (*Dei Verbum*, par. 25; quoted in the *Catechism*, par. 133). The Council went on to quote St. Jerome, who lived around A.D. 400: "Ignorance of the Scriptures is ignorance of Christ."

Approaching Scripture prayerfully, with a listening heart, is different from studying it as we would a history book or a catechism. There's certainly a place for study. In fact, as a theology professor, I make my living by giving people the historical, doctrinal, academic foundation they need to read and understand Scripture. As helpful as this is for laying the groundwork for prayer, however, it's not what you do in prayer itself.

When we come to the Bible in prayer, we're looking more for formation than *in*formation. We read it as God's personal word to us—like a love letter, as many people have said. The Bible is where we meet God and experience him nourishing, challenging, guiding, and speaking to us on a day-by-day basis. The first step to reading Scripture prayerfully, then, is to ask the Spirit to open up its meaning to us. Since the Spirit inspired the words of Scripture, he can inspire us to understand and be formed by them.

The inspiration of Scripture doesn't just mean that the Spirit guided the people who wrote it hundreds of years ago. Scripture is God-breathed; the Spirit actually dwells in the inspired word. This is why many of the Church Fathers spoke of Scripture as a temple of the Holy Spirit. As we reverently enter this temple, we give ourselves an opportunity to be touched by the living Word of God and empowered by his Spirit.

Certain questions should always accompany our reading: What is God saying to me today through this text? What does he want me to do? How is he challenging me? How am I to apply this in my life? If we listen as we read, we will surely come to "the surpassing worth of knowing Christ Jesus" (Phil 3:8) at work in us.

There are different ways of reading Scripture. Some people

choose a biblical book and go straight through it by reading a chapter or two a day. This continuous reading has a long history of fruitfulness. It's the basic approach behind the lectionary readings at Mass during the "ordinary times" of the liturgical year. Any Catholic who attends Sunday Mass over the course of three years (or daily Mass over the course of two years) will hear all the main passages of the Bible.

Another way to read the Bible is to focus on just one text—maybe a passage that has leapt out at you and gotten your attention. Get into it. Chomp on it, chew it over like a cow chews its cud. This is precisely what the early monks meant when they talked about "ruminating" on the word of God. It's the approach taken by *Focolare*, a movement in the Church whose members all take the same Scripture verse to think over and live out over the course of a month. What a great practice!

There's no need to worry about our supply of scriptural nourishment ever running out. Because the Word comes from the eternal God, it has a limitless ability to address and feed us. Even after we've assimilated a text and let it become part of us, we can return to it again and again with a sense of expectation.

Focusing on an individual text naturally leads to memorizing it, which is a traditionally Catholic thing to do. The early Fathers of the Church had most of the Scriptures memorized. So did later saints like Anthony of Padua. If you put together all the Bible verses recited from memory in his open-air sermons, you'd have pretty much the whole Bible!

Helps for Tuning in to God's Word

Various aids can help us read Scripture prayerfully. We can keep up with Mass readings by consulting a missal. There are many helpful books, as well as monthly magazines that help Catholics understand and apply the Word of God (some examples are *Magnificat, God's Word Today,* and *The Word Among Us*).

Another great encouragement, and an important part of hearing God in the Catholic tradition, is to look at God's word as it's illustrated in the lives of people who took it seriously and lived it to the hilt. These are the saints.

One reason for investigating the saints is that they shed light on the meaning of Scripture. Let's face it: Scripture isn't always easy to understand. We can easily sympathize with the Ethiopian eunuch we meet in the Acts of the Apostles—the person that Philip is sent to meet on the Gaza road. The man is sitting in his chariot reading Isaiah's prophecy about Jesus, the "suffering servant," but he's not getting it. "Do you understand what you are reading?" Philip asks. And the Ethiopian replies, "How can I unless, some one guides me?" (see Acts 8:26-40.)

Verbal explanations of a Scripture text, like the one Philip gives the eunuch, sometimes figure in saints' biographies. Generally, though, their lives themselves function as a running commentary that illustrates God's word in action. For me, this reading has been a critical part of my spiritual growth. Lives of people who love God in a heroic way challenge and stimulate me. They give me ideas on how to put into practice what the Lord is telling me.

Padre Pio was the first person to affect me this way. Right after my teenage conversion, someone gave me a biography of this twentieth-century Italian priest. Going into that book, I was a rock musician. Coming out of it, I wanted to give everything away and follow Jesus without compromise. I went on to discover St. Francis of Assisi, Padre Pio's model, and then many other holy men and women.

Now that I'm married with five children and can't just give everything away, the married saint Sir Thomas More has been a guiding light. On a recent trip to England, both my appreciation for St. Thomas and my love for Jesus were increased as I visited the Tower of London, where Thomas was imprisoned before his execution. There, as he awaited death, he wrote about Jesus' agony in the garden; he pondered Jesus' fear and trembling and his resolve to be faithful to his Father's will regardless of the cost. Who could possibly have more insight into this text than a man on the verge of execution, who was living this mystery himself?

I use a prayer journal to help me remember insights gained from reading the lives of the saints and Scripture. I've found this a tremendous help in listening to God. My approach is simple. Every day I try to write down whatever God speaks to me through Scripture or other reading, whatever inspiration I receive in the course of the day's events, thoughts, and conversations. After a few weeks I review it.

My discoveries amaze me sometimes. I find patterns. I see encouraging words I've forgotten or challenges I've pushed aside. In short, keeping a prayer journal is an effective way to gather up the bread of the word and not lose a morsel.

Biblical Prayers for Your Prayer Time

How do we respond to the Lord once we've listened to him? The most traditional way is by using the psalms, the scriptural prayers inspired by the Holy Spirit. The *Catechism* calls these "the masterwork of prayer in the Old Testament" (par. 2596). Indeed the Church has always found the Psalms to be its very best prayer book. In the Liturgy of the Hours, or "divine office," the psalms are arranged into prayers for morning, evening, and other times of day. Over its four-week cycle, the Liturgy of the Hours includes almost all of the 150 psalms.

If you don't feel ready for the Liturgy of the Hours, you might simply make it a habit to pray one or two psalms a day. Gradually, you'll find your own prayer being shaped by the psalms' inspired patterns. The psalms will also provide you with prayers for every mood and situation. There are psalms for the days when you're exultant and full of praise. When you're dejected, lonely, or overwhelmed, you'll find psalms that give voice to those feelings too.

There are many other great biblical prayers. The first two chapters of Luke's Gospel offer three "canticles," or songs of praise. One is the *Magnificat,* Mary's response to Elizabeth's exclamation, "Who am I, that the mother of my Lord should come to me?" Instead of saying, "Yeah, I'm really great and important," Mary gave all the praise to God with her humble but glorious prayer, "My soul magnifies the Lord...." (see Lk 1:46-55). Every day the Catholic Church prays the *Magnificat* in its evening prayer. Another canticle appears in its morning prayer. This one is from Elizabeth's husband, Zechariah, whose muteness vanished in a burst of praise when John the Baptist was born (see Lk 1:68-79). The Church's night prayer includes the canticle of Simeon, the old man who waited his whole life to see the Messiah whom Mary and Joseph brought to the temple in swaddling clothes (see Lk 2:29-32).

Of course, the Bible's best-known prayer is the Our Father, which is the pattern of all Christian prayer. The *Catechism,* which devotes one of its four parts to the subject of prayer, gives a good extended commentary on the Our Father (see pars. 2759-2865). Look it over and you'll understand why the Lord's Prayer has been called "the summary of the whole gospel" as well as "the most perfect of prayers" (Tertullian and Thomas Aquinas quoted in the *Catechism,* par. 2774).

Contrary to what some think, the Hail Mary is biblical, too. This prayer is mainly composed of two quotations from the Gospel of Luke. "Hail, Mary, full of grace; the Lord is with you" comes from the angel's greeting to Mary (see Lk 1:28). "Blessed are you among women, and blessed is the fruit of your womb!" is from Elizabeth's greeting (Lk 1:42).

The Our Father and Hail Mary come together in the rosary. Interestingly, in the rosary these structured prayers direct our attention not so much to their own words as to the "mysteries," the events surrounding Jesus' birth, suffering, death, resurrection, ascension, and sending of the Spirit. To pray the rosary is to meditate on these great deeds of the Lord together with Mary, who pondered all these things in her heart (see Lk 2:19). The rosary's Hail Marys and Our Fathers form a sort of background—like tapping your foot to the music—that engages you as your mind focuses on the mysteries. As many saints, popes, and other spiritual writers have taught, it's better to pray one decade of the rosary and meditate on its scriptural mystery than to crank out fifteen decades mechanically and without reflection.

Thanksgiving: A Prayer Always in Season

Maybe you've come across the popular acronym—ACTS—that sums up various types of responses to God in prayer. It stands for Adoration, Confession, Thanksgiving, and Supplication. While each of these aspects is important, I'd like to highlight thanksgiving, which plays a key role in leading us to joy and keeping us rooted in the Lord.

For Catholics, the main ceremony of the Christian life is the liturgy of the Eucharist, which takes its name from the Greek word meaning "to thank." Fundamentally, the Eucharist is a thanksgiving for all that God has done for us—"for all his benefits, for all that he has accomplished through creation, redemption, and sanctification," as the *Catechism* explains (par. 1360). Truly, thanksgiving is meant to color the entire Christian life.

Thanksgiving has some pretty amazing effects. For one, it takes our eyes off self and focuses them on God. It counteracts our tendency to keep asking for more and to get preoccupied by our needs and lacks. The result is growth in true humility—not its "down on yourself" counterfeit, but the virtue by which we look to God and don't think of ourselves at all.

Two of the three prayers of Jesus whose words are recorded in the New Testament are prayers of thanksgiving (see Mt 11:25; Jn 11:41). Also, notice that "give us this day our daily bread" isn't the first petition of the prayer Jesus taught us. Only towards the end of the Our Father do we pray for our needs.

First we pray, "hallowed be thy name"—Father, may your name be held holy. This is praise and adoration, along with thanksgiving.

Praise and thanksgiving are not only related; they're inseparable. Praise focuses on who God is, in and of himself. Thanksgiving has to do with our response to the benefits God has given us. But the two are intertwined. How can we know God's greatness, glory, and mercy except through his gifts and actions toward us?

Psalm 34:5 says, "Look to God that you may be radiant with joy" (NAB). In thanksgiving and praise we look to God, and that produces tremendous joy.

If you want joy, cultivate the habit of thanking God for everything, as St. Paul advises: "Rejoice always, pray constantly, give thanks in all circumstances" (1 Thes 5:16-18). This is hard sometimes. It's challenging to give thanks in the midst of auto accidents, traffic jams, serious illness, and other unpleasant situations. But in faith we know that "in everything God works for good with those who love him" (Rom 8:28).

Take the Challenge

God's plan for us corresponds with our own natural desire for joy and happiness. But where we might settle for the feelings of euphoria that often accompany conversion and new life in Christ, God wants nothing less for us than profound joy that no one can take away.

It's like what happens in marriage. For every couple, the challenge is to move from the carefree joy of the honeymoon to the nitty-gritty of "real life" in a way that deepens and develops love. That kind of transition needs to happen in our relationship with God, too. Persistent personal prayer is the key. Without a disciplined, sustained conversation with the Lord in daily prayer, we won't know the joys of a mature spiritual life.

I'm not going to kid you: prayer is hard work. Sometimes it's agony. Look at Jesus' agony in the garden. That wasn't playacting. It was for real. Whatever it may cost us, though, prayer is worth the struggle. Over time, it really does yield holiness, intimacy, and joy.

Wherever we are in our personal prayer life, let's make a decision to move on. But let's be realistic. Our goal isn't to become mystics overnight. Let's simply identify and take the next step in the journey of personal prayer, the journey that leads to intimacy with the Lord and true joy.

Chapter Five

What Is the Mass?

Even Catholics who don't know much about their faith are vaguely aware that they're supposed to go to Mass on Sunday. Ask them to describe the Mass, though, and they might tell you that it involves an introduction, a conclusion, and a collection!

The Mass (also called the Eucharist or the Divine Liturgy) has two main parts, the Liturgy of the Word and the Liturgy of the Eucharist. But rather than analyze its parts, I'd like to examine the Mass as a whole in terms of its three principal aspects. Now and always, the Mass involves a *sacrifice, the presence of Christ,* and a *meal.*

The Sacrifice That Transcends Time

It's important to know what the church means by the "sacrifice" of the Mass. The term is easily misunderstood and has caused much strife among Christians.

First of all, church teaching reiterates what Scripture states very clearly: there is no other sacrifice except the one offered by Jesus on Calvary. Hebrews 10:12 says that Christ "offered for all time a single sacrifice for sins." That sacrifice cannot be repeated. The Mass, therefore, is not a repetition; it is a *re-presentation* of that sacrifice.

Because Christ was a unique human being, the sacrifice he offered on the cross once and for all is a unique act. He was a human being, so it was an act that took place in history and is therefore past. He is God, who is outside of time: past and future are always present to him. This means that his death and resurrection are eternal acts that can be made present by the power of the Spirit.

This is exactly what happens in the Eucharist. The power of Calvary—the sacrifice that takes away sins, heals, and transforms—becomes present and available to us. It can be applied to our need.

But that's not all. The cross is incomplete without the Resurrection. You can't understand what happened on Good Friday apart from what happened two days later on Easter Sunday. This means that the Resurrection, too, is made present every time the Eucharist is celebrated. When we go to Mass, we're present at the foot of the cross, watching the Savior give his life for us. And we're outside the open tomb with the risen Jesus and the women who greeted him on that resurrection morning. "This is for you. I give my life to you," Jesus is saying. "Receive my power."

Jesus offered himself as a sacrifice in order to bring us salvation and give us his Spirit. Pentecost is the fruit of the sacrifice of the cross and the victory of the Resurrection. Thus, the church teaches that every Mass is a new Pentecost, a new opportunity to receive the Spirit afresh (see the *Catechism of the Catholic Church*, par. 739).

To sum up, the Mass is Christ's sacrifice made present again. It's not recalled, as if it had been absent or were merely a past event. It's re-presented.

Giving Thanks, Giving Ourselves

In a very real way, the Eucharist is *our* sacrifice, too. The New Testament calls us "priests," and priests are those who offer sacrifice. "Like living stones be yourselves built into a spiritual house, to be a holy priesthood, to offer spiritual sacrifices acceptable to God through Jesus Christ" (1 Pt 2:5). If there is only one sacrifice, then somehow our priesthood associates us with Christ's act of self-offering to the Father.

The Mass is also *our* sacrifice in that we join our own offerings to Christ's. First, we offer a sacrifice of praise and thanks. "Eucharist means first of all 'thanksgiving,'" says the *Catechism* (par. 1360). We thank the Lord for his sacrifice, which is for us and our salvation. In the Eucharistic Prayer, a long prayer of thanks to the Father uttered toward the middle of every Mass, the celebrant speaks for us all. He thanks God for the creation of the world and for its goodness; he prays in thanksgiving for salvation history, for the whole human race is offered salvation through Jesus' coming, death, and Resurrection.

During the Eucharistic Prayer, I always silently add in thanks for my personal blessings. I think of the natural blessings of home and work, of food on the table and the health of my family. I also thank God for my own salvation history, especially for plucking me out of danger I was heading into as a teenager—a journey that led many of my friends into drug and alcohol abuse. I thank God for bringing me together with a woman who loves him and loves me, and for having kept us faithful to him and each other for many years. I thank him for our own family's salvation history.

If you haven't already established the habit of adding your

personalized thank-yous to the priest's Eucharistic Prayer, try it next time you're at Mass. It's a very appropriate mode of participating in that part of the Eucharist.

But our Eucharistic sacrifice involves more than offering thanks for what God has done. It means offering *ourselves* in response to his self-gift. Note what Paul says in his letter to the Romans: "I appeal to you therefore, brethren, by the mercies of God, to present your bodies as a living sacrifice, holy and acceptable to God, which is your spiritual worship" (Rom 12:1).

In a way, this is what the animal sacrifices of the Old Testament symbolized. Animals were very precious to the Israelites, and only the best were considered worthy for offering to God. These unblemished, perfect animals represented—even substituted for—the life of the person who offered them. Sacrificing them was a sign of the worshiper's complete gift of self to the Lord.

This brings us to the collection at Mass! Believe it or not, the collection is really important. Whether we put in the widow's mite or have the means to give much more, our financial contribution represents the gift of ourselves. As it's brought forward at the presentation of the gifts, along with the bread and wine, our financial contribution serves as a sign of our self-offering.

It has to be said that many of us don't give much of ourselves in the Eucharist. As a result, we don't receive much back. The solution is to stop being the audience and learn to be actors in the drama of the Eucharistic sacrifice, as the Second Vatican Council exhorted us: "The laity at Mass should not be silent spectators. Offering the Immaculate Victim [that is, Christ] not only through the hands of the priest but also together with him, they should learn to offer themselves ("Constitution on the Sacred Liturgy," *Sacrosanctum Concilium* 48). And here's a beautiful statement on the subject from Fr. Johannes Emminghaus, a German scholar: "In the Eucharist the church enters into this total self-giving of Christ, and we individually attempt to enter into it as fully as possible. Merely to go through the motions of the Mass without this serious and complete gift of self would simply be hypocrisy" (J. Emminghaus, *Eucharist: Essence, Form, and Celebration,* 2nd ed. (Collegeville: Liturgical Press, 1978, xxi).

Offering thanks to the Lord and giving our whole selves to the Father together with Christ is what the eucharistic sacrifice is about. Obviously, we are weak and our sacrifice is imperfect. Nevertheless, during the preparation of the gifts, we should be putting everything important to us on the altar. This includes our precious treasures of time, ambitions, desires, relationships, work accomplishments, family matters, trials, and temptations.

These are our contributions, but the sacrifice is still Christ's. How could it be otherwise, since we died when we were baptized? "It is no longer I who live, but Christ who lives in me; and the life I now live in the flesh I live by faith in the Son of God," says St. Paul (Gal 2:20). Anything that's of merit or value in our lives is really Christ working through us.

Our offerings are added, then, to the personal sacrifice of Christ our head, giving us the privilege of sharing in his sacrifice to the Father. This is symbolized beautifully just before the consecration, when the priest mixes a small amount of water with the wine. The paltry sacrifice that is our life is like the water that is absorbed into the rich sacrifice of Christ, which is symbolized by the wine.

Really Present in Priest and People

Whether they're Catholic or not, whether they understand it or not, most people have heard the term, "the real presence," and know it has something to do with what Catholics believe about the Mass. Indeed, the church teaches that Christ is really present in the Eucharist—and present in at least four different ways.

First, Christ is present *in the congregation.* Jesus said he's there whenever two or three are gathered in his name (see Mt 18:20), and usually the Sunday Mass congregation numbers more than two or three! Even when it's hard to see Christ in our fellow Mass-goers, he's really there. People may arrive distracted and preoccupied, but as they enter that church they're no longer just scattered individuals but members of Christ's body. Whether conscious of it or not, they're being drawn together into the body of Christ.

At Mass we deepen our communion with the whole church, as well as with the Lord. That's what the sign of peace is about. Though sometimes viewed as a trendy idea inserted into the Mass around 1970, the sign of peace is really a recovery of a practice of the early church. It recalls what Jesus said in Matthew 5:23-24: "If you are offering your gift at the altar, and there remember that your brother has something against you, leave your gift before the altar and go; first be reconciled to your brother, and then come and offer your gift." The sign of peace is intended not so much as an opportunity for back-slapping fellowship as a sign that we hold nothing against anyone. It means we renounce all bitterness, resentment, and jealousy as we come as one body to receive the Lord together.

Often, our conscience is clear about not having committed any sins against the people in the congregation. We haven't backed into someone's car and not informed them, nor have we defamed anyone, robbed or defrauded. But along with sins of *commission*, it's important to take note of our sins of *omission*.

In his first letter to the church in Corinth, Paul upbraided the Corinthians for what they were *failing* to do. Apparently, there were rich members of the congregation who were oblivious to the needs of the poor members. They'd eat a magnificent meal while the poor sat there hungry and thirsty, and afterward rich and poor would all come together to celebrate the Eucharist. That's seriously wrong, Paul told them. In fact, "that is why many of you are weak and ill, and some have died" (1 Cor 11:30).

"Discerning the body," as Paul put it—discerning the fact that the community is Christ's body in a very real way—is a serious matter. Christ is present in our fellow worshipers at Mass, and what we do or don't do to the least of them, we do or don't do to Christ (see Mt 25:40, 45).

Second, Christ is present at Mass *in the person of the priest*. It's not a question of whether the ordained minister is an exciting preacher or a particularly holy person. Many of our priests are, in fact, inspiring in holiness and powerful in their preaching. Others are not. But the good news is that Christ's presence doesn't depend on the priest's personal virtue. Christ makes himself present through the charism that the priest has been given through ordination. This is one of the reasons that the Catholic priest wears vestments when he celebrates the Eucharist: it signifies that he's acting in the person of Christ, not in his own person.

Actually, Jesus is the only priest. Thomas Aquinas put it straightforwardly: "Only Christ is the true priest, the others being only his ministers" (*Catechism*, par. 1545). The ordained priest is an icon or image of Christ. Through him, Jesus makes his priesthood present in a very special way.

If you're happy with your parish priest, if his celebration of the Mass moves you, that's a tremendous blessing. Thank God for him! If he's less than inspiring and somehow makes it harder for you to pray, then pray for him. Priests have an awesome responsibility and a very difficult job. All of them deserve our loving support.

One of the things I love about St. Francis of Assisi is that he never took potshots at the clergy. In an age of widespread clerical corruption, Francis always thanked God for being able to receive the sacred Body and Blood from the hands of a priest, whether worthy or unworthy. More effectively than denunciations, Francis's loving example brought about a change in many priests, calling them to greater virtue and deeper life in Christ.

Jesus, the Living Word

Third, the Lord is present in the Eucharist *in the Word of God*. It's a caricature to depict the Protestant church as the church of the Word and the Catholic Church as the church of the sacraments. This is certainly not the case.

The Catholic Church sees the Bible, the inspired word of God, as a priceless gift, and this is reflected in the Eucharist. In fact, the first part of the Mass centers around readings from Scripture: one passage, a psalm response, sometimes another passage, and then a reading from one of the gospels.

This Liturgy of the Word isn't an abstract catechism lesson. Through the readings, the Lord wants to speak to us personally, cutting through all our defenses and penetrating to the depths of our hearts with a nourishing, challenging word leading us to conversion. This has happened time and time again in the church's history.

Francis Bernardone, son of a cloth merchant in Assisi, walked into church one day during a period when he was searching for meaning in life. He opened the lectionary to this text: "Go, sell what you have, and give to the poor,... and come, follow me" (Mk 10:21). Francis knew this word wasn't just for the apostles 1200 years earlier; it was for him, right there and then. He walked out of church, did exactly what that Scripture said, and so began a world-wide spiritual revolution that still impacts us today.

My own conversion began in a similar way. I had never missed Sunday Mass except when ill, but it didn't mean a whole lot to me. I kept showing up, though, and because I was there, the Spirit suddenly one Sunday gave me ears to hear. The gospel reading—Jesus' calling Peter to come and follow him—penetrated to the depths of my being. I was so impressed that I ripped out the reading from the missalette, took it home, and put it up on my wall. I started reading Scripture, and before long my life was transformed.

This is how the Lord wants to work in our lives. We can cooperate by cultivating openness to the word heard at Mass.

It's not just at the table of the Eucharist that we're nourished. The pulpit is like a table, too, as the Second Vatican Council explains: "The Church has always venerated the divine Scriptures just as she venerates the body of the Lord, since from the table of both the word of God and of the body of Christ she unceasingly receives and offers to the faithful the bread of life, especially in the sacred liturgy" (*Dei verbum,* par. 21). We read the Scriptures first because they build up our faith. Christ is present in them, preparing us to discern the real presence of his body and blood under the signs of bread and wine.

In addition to the readings, the word of God comes to us through the prayers of Mass. Listen carefully, and you'll discover that these prayers are almost entirely scriptural. They're either direct quotes or paraphrases like the Creed, which the Church Fathers put together as a summary of the essential Scriptures.

Take the greeting that the priest usually gives us when he walks in: "[May] the grace of our Lord Jesus Christ, and the love of God and the fellowship of the Holy Spirit be with you all." That's a direct quote from St. Paul: 2 Corinthians 13:14. Or the *Gloria* that we pray on most Sundays: "Glory to God in the highest and peace to his people on earth." That's from Luke 2:14. At every Mass we sing "Holy, holy, holy, Lord, God of power and might." That's from Isaiah 6:3, with a bit of another Scripture passage thrown in toward the end. What about "Behold, the Lamb of God, who takes away the sin of the world"? That's what John the Baptist said (Jn 1:29). And then there's my favorite, that great Italian, the centurion who told the Lord he wasn't worthy to welcome him under his roof (see Mt 8:8); we quote him every time we pray, "Lord, I am not worthy to receive you...."

This Is My Body, My Blood

The final and most special way that the Lord is present in the Eucharist is *in his Body and Blood*, present to us under the signs of bread and wine.

Jesus is God, and so he is omnipresent. But Jesus is man as well as God; his humanity can't be present everywhere in the same way as his divinity. Jesus' glorified humanity is at the right hand of the Father. In the Eucharist and only in the Eucharist, though, he makes his Body and Blood present to us in a totally real way. This is why the sacramental presence of Christ's Body and Blood is so extraordinary. In all of the other sacraments Jesus gives us his grace, says St. Thomas Aquinas, while in the Eucharist, the "sacrament of sacraments," he gives us his whole self, his divinity and his humanity.

How is this possible? How can Jesus be present bodily under the forms of bread and wine? Many people have the impression that it's all hocus-pocus. But the Eucharist is emphatically not magic. Rather, the transformation of bread and wine into Christ's body and blood happens the same way Mary's virginal conception did: through the power of the Word and the overshadowing of the Spirit (Lk 1:26–38). The incarnation may seem impossible, yet all Christians believe it. It happens the same way creation did: God spoke, the wind of the Spirit moved, and the chaos was transformed into creation (Gn 1). Likewise, in the Eucharist, the One who said "Let there be light" says "This is my Body" and "This is my Blood." Through the power of the Spirit invoked upon the gifts, an awesome change takes place.

About the year 1200 or so, as some Catholics were struggling to find a way to explain this change, they came up with the word "transubstantiation." Many people struggle with this word today! One reason why we find it hard to understand is that the word "substance" has different meanings. For us, substance is something you can touch. Substance abuse, for example, has to do with tangibles like drugs and alcohol. In theology, though, substance means something that *underlies* what you can see and touch; it's the essence of the thing that resides under its appearances. Surface characteristics—"accidents," as theologians call them—have to do with everything that could be otherwise—say, how long your hair is or how fat or thin you are.

Transubstantiation, therefore, means that while everything looks the same on the surface, the underlying essence of a thing is changed. This is just the opposite of what happens in the world we see. Usually, appearances change while the essence of a thing stays the same. In the Eucharist, though, the underlying, invisible substance is transformed from bread and wine to Christ's Body and Blood. Everything looks the same as before. Even with a microscope, you wouldn't be able to tell the difference, for the level at which this change happens is far too deep for human probing. But in the Eucharist, Christ is as truly present in his Body, Blood, soul, and divinity as when he walked the roads of Galilee, healing and preaching.

A Meal Like No Other

The Eucharist is a meal. It's the Lord's Supper, as well as a holy sacrifice. It has to be both. Christ becomes present so that we can not only see him under the appearances of bread and wine but also receive him into ourselves. Very tangibly, he becomes our food.

Food is very important in Christianity. I'm happy about that, because as an Italian, food is important to me! But even those of us who deeply appreciate food might wonder why the Lord chose to make himself present in this particular way. Why bread and wine?

Bread is our basic daily nourishment. The Our Father's "Give us this day our daily bread" is a petition for all our needs and necessities. The Fathers of the Church also understood it as a prayer for the spiritual nourishment we need on a daily basis—the Eucharist and the word of God.

If you want to understand the Eucharist, slowly read and pray your way through the sixth chapter of John's Gospel. That's where Jesus tells the crowd, "I am the bread of life," presenting himself as the bread "which comes down from heaven, and gives life to the world" (Jn 6:35, 33). His words connect the Eucharist with the manna that God rained down from heaven to sustain the people of Israel on their Exodus journey. Manna, too, has a deeper spiritual significance, because God provided it for more than the people's physical survival. The book of Deuteronomy says it was also to show them that "man does not live by bread alone," but by every word that comes from the mouth of God (Dt 8:3). Bread, then, is the sign of our daily nourishment, both physical and spiritual.

Wine is the blood of the grape, obtainable only by crushing the grape. It symbolizes the cup of suffering, the price Jesus paid for us so that we might be free. From this cup we, too, must drink, if we are to be his disciples. Remember the mother of James and John who requests a favor for her sons? "Hey Jesus, can you honor them with a special place on your right and left?" she wants to know. Jesus responds by asking the two a sobering question: "Are you able to drink the cup that I am to drink?" (Mt 20:22). Whatever seating assignment they end up with, he assures them, they will not escape this cup of suffering.

Wine also symbolizes the cup of joy. In both Old Testament and New Testament times, wine was associated with festivity and special celebrations. "Wine ... cheers gods and men" and serves to "gladden the heart of man" (Jgs 9:13; Ps 104:15). The wedding feast of Cana is a good example. By evoking suffering, wine points back to Jesus' death on the cross; by evoking joy, it points forward to the messianic banquet in heaven.

The symbol of wine—the blood of the grape that becomes the Blood of Jesus—is even richer in light of the Old Testament. There, blood is equated with life. It's not seen as sustaining life; rather, for the Jew, blood *is* life, and it belongs to God alone. It's for this reason that the Mosaic Law forbids drinking blood or eating any animal that still has blood in it. Even today, Jews who keep a kosher table only eat animals that have been appropriately butchered and drained of all blood.

In the Eucharist, Jesus gives us a share in God's divine life by giving us his own blood. His plan for us goes way beyond making us into decent folks who are scrubbed up and clean of gross immorality. Jesus came so that we might share in everything he has and become "partakers of the divine nature" (2 Pt 1:4).

What is this divine nature? Essentially, it's the inner life of the Trinity: three Persons eternally pouring themselves out in self-giving love for each other. This is *agape*, or charity, and drinking Jesus' Blood gives us an opportunity to share in it. "I came that they may have life, and have it abundantly," Jesus assures us (Jn 10:10). Let's not settle for just a tiny taste!

In order for us to stay alive, every cell in our body needs to be bathed with the blood that nourishes, cleanses, and purifies our system. Similarly, taking the Blood of Christ in Communion will bring us to full spiritual vitality. It will strengthen and cleanse our entire being—spiritually and even physically, if it be God's will.

The One we take upon our lips and into our bodies in the Eucharist is the same Jesus who raised Lazarus and healed the man born blind. Do we think about this enough? At Communion we receive Jesus, the risen Lord who will come again in glory to judge the living and the dead. Do we come to him with faith that he can totally transform and heal us? When I go to Communion, I'm conscious of the spiritual sickness in my life and sometimes of physical needs, and I ask Jesus to heal and change me. I beg him not to let me walk out of church the same person as I walked in.

In every culture I know, sharing a meal with someone is a way of expressing and deepening a relational bond. The Eucharist does this in a way no other meal can. We eat with God, he gives himself as our food, and we're transformed into him. When we receive him and consume him under these signs of bread and wine, we *become* him. What intimacy! What mystery!

The Eucharist is a great deal. Consider the exchange we're invited to make. We come forward, put our humble gifts on the altar—our little sacrifices, imperfect good works, our need and brokenness—and what do we get back in return? We receive the Lord's own life, bursting with power to heal and transform us.

In the Eucharist Jesus holds absolutely nothing back from us. He gives us his entire self. May we, in the Eucharist, learn to return the favor and give him both everything we have and everything we are.

Chapter Six

Getting More out of the Mass

If Christ really shows up at every Mass, why do so many walk out apparently no better off than when they walked in? The power that moves mountains, raised Lazarus from the dead, and created heaven and earth is present in the liturgy. Shouldn't Mass-goers, then, be experiencing more changes in their lives?

This seeming lack of results proves to some that Catholic teaching about Christ's real presence in the Eucharist can't be right. But there are two sides to church teaching on the subject, and both must be understood if we're to have a balanced picture.

On the one hand, Christ is truly present in the Eucharist. He's among us just as truly as he walked amidst the crowds during his public ministry. On the other hand, the fruit that we're supposed to bear as a result of Christ's Eucharistic presence is directly proportional to the level of faith and love we bring with us to Mass. I think this point needs to be better understood, because it explains why so few appear changed by the Eucharist. It all comes down to one question: how open are we to the presence of the Lord?

It's Our Choice

Jesus is a lover who doesn't force himself on anyone. This is as true for us as it was for the first-century residents of Jerusalem. We often think, "If only I'd lived back then, I'd have more faith. Seeing Jesus with my own eyes would remove all my doubts."

Really? Just look at how people in the Gospels responded to Jesus. Think about the crowd that Jesus walked through the time he whirled around and said, "Who touched me?" (see Mk 5:24-34). The apostles didn't get it. "What are you saying, Jesus? Here all these people are bumping into you, and you want to know who touched you?" But Jesus meant, "Who touched me with faith?" This, of course, was the woman with the hemorrhage, who had bled for years, wasting all of her money on doctors. Of the whole multitude who had had physical contact with Jesus, she was the only one healed. No one else recognized who Jesus was. They expected nothing, and they got nothing.

Look at what happened when Jesus returned to his hometown of Nazareth. Did his friends and neighbors give him a rousing welcome? On the contrary. Matthew says that Jesus "did not do many mighty works there, because of their unbelief." Mark says: "He was not able to perform any mighty deed there, apart from curing a few people by laying hands on them. He was amazed at their lack of faith" (Mt 13:58; Mk 6:5-6, NAB). This last Scripture startled me so much that I had to go back and reread it several times. The message is sobering: Jesus is omnipotent, but he chooses not to work where people aren't open to him.

When I try to think of a good image for this, I think of what the summer sun does to the soil in Texas. We get very little rain then, so by mid-June the ground is baked as hard as clay pottery. Whenever we do get the occasional downpour, the water can't soak in because the ground hasn't been prepared. It just runs off. That's what happens with many of us at Mass. Grace is available, but we're not able to receive it. We're not ready. Our hearts are hard and haven't been broken up through prayer, faith, and fasting. That's really the problem.

When we approach the Mass without active faith in Jesus' presence, we're pretty much in the same boat as the unbelieving people of Nazareth. They saw a carpenter, an ordinary man. They didn't see God, and neither do we. "*This* congregation is Christ's Body?" we ask incredulously. "Why, I know these folks. They talk behind each other's backs, they cheat on their income taxes.... Christ is present in *this* priest? You've got to be joking!... He's present when the word is read? That lector can barely put together a coherent English sentence.... And Communion? I see bread and wine, not God."

Even if we *say* we believe in Christ's eucharistic presence, our words ring hollow if we don't express this faith by our actions. "You Catholics are ridiculous," a non-Catholic friend once told one of my students. She had observed how nonchalantly many of us approach the Mass, and it just didn't add up. "If I believed what you say you believe," she said, "I'd be crawling to that tabernacle every day on my hands and knees to be with the One you say is in there."

The question we need to ask ourselves is this: Does the way in which I approach the Mass—my preparation, conduct, and follow-up—reflect true belief that here, in this event, I encounter the King of Kings and Lord of Lords? Does my attitude indicate that Sunday Eucharist is the high point of my entire week?

Probably most of us have to admit that there's room for improvement in this area. With this in mind, I've come up with a few specific strategies for how to make the Eucharist—especially on Sunday—a more fruitful experience, regardless of the particulars of the priest, choir, and congregation.

Before Mass Begins

Preparing by fasting. The church has a discipline of a Eucharistic fast. For Latin rite Catholics, this means an obligation to abstain from everything but water for one hour prior to receiving Communion. This minimal requirement serves to remind us that the Eucharistic banquet is an event to prepare for.

Certainly, we're free to do more. For example, we might consider blocking out media-generated distractions. Why not leave the radio and TV off, the newspaper unopened, and the computer idle for an hour or more before the Eucharist. That way, our minds are freer of noise and clutter, and we don't have to spend our entire time in church fighting against distractions.

Pondering the readings. We can prepare for Mass by looking over the biblical readings ahead of time. This gives us a head start in understanding and digesting them before we hear them read aloud in church.

Preparing by praying. The church has always recommended that we prepare for Mass through prayer. One way to do this is to get to Mass a little early. Even five minutes can give you time to dial down, unwind a bit, and focus on the Lord.

Whenever I get to church early enough for this prayer time, I concentrate on arousing my faith. I make conscious acts of faith in Christ's manifold presence in the liturgy. My prayer might go something like this: "Lord, I see these folks around me. Some of them are distracted; others I don't necessarily like, on a human level. But I believe that these are your brothers and sisters, and therefore mine. Together, we are one body in you. I honor you here.... Lord, I believe that today's celebrant is really acting in your place and that you're exercising your priesthood through him. Empower his preaching today. Help him to participate reverently in this Eucharist.... Lord, I believe you're going to be present in the word. Open my ears to hear you. I don't want to be daydreaming about my to-do list. I don't want to come away with ideas that don't affect how I live. Make it possible for me to focus—to hear and respond to you.... Finally, Lord, help me to see and worship you as I receive your sacred Body and Blood...."

Praying through these things is a way of exercising our faith muscles. It's rather like working out. You really can't grow your muscles unless you exercise them.

I have to admit that this quiet, recollected time of prayer works best for me on weekdays. On Sundays, when Susan and I attend Mass with our five children, it's just not a possibility. But we do try to prepare as a family while driving to church. We sing a few songs and offer spontaneous prayers like, "Lord, help us to concentrate at this Eucharist. We want to give ourselves to you." I don't want to give the impression that this works perfectly. Sometimes, it's really chaotic! Still, we make the effort, and maybe half the time we actually succeed in having some recollected prayer. Even when it doesn't work out, it teaches the children that Mass is important and requires preparation.

Dressing for the occasion. When I first started coming to terms with the reality of Christ's Eucharistic presence, I realized that the way I dressed for Sunday Mass didn't reflect my belief. Being something of a hippie at the time, I often walked into church wearing cut-off jeans and tank top t-shirts. "What do my clothes matter?" I used to think. But then it occurred to me that perhaps they weren't really appropriate, given the magnitude of the event. Without shopping for a wardrobe of designer suits, I did start dressing more respectfully in honor of the occasion.

For sure, I'd never encourage anyone to get into a competition about who's best-dressed at Mass. I do think it's worth asking this question, though: Does the way I dress for Sunday Mass reflect my faith that I'm visiting Christ and that this is the central event of my week?

Deciding about the kids. Parents of young children should know that there's no law about coming to Mass as a family. You're perfectly free to attend together or to split up, depending on what works best.

Sometimes, "divide and conquer" is the best approach. When we had three kids under three, it was hopeless for all five of us to go to the Sunday Eucharist together. Whenever we tried it, Susan and I ended up spending the entire time trying to keep the children from ruining everyone else's recollection. For quite a while, we just traded off and didn't go to Sunday Mass together unless we had a relative or friend to babysit. That way, each of us—to say nothing of the rest of the congregation—could have a recollected time of prayer at Mass.

The point is that parents have to exercise both flexibility and determination so that each one can prepare for Mass and experience it prayerfully. This requires creativity. Right now in my family, I'm often away on Sundays and my wife has to take all five kids to church. One solution to this is for me to cover for her during the week so that she can get to at least one daily Mass by herself. If that's impossible, we try to arrange it so that she spends an hour before the Blessed Sacrament. That way, she can unpack what she received but was unable to think about during the Sunday Eucharist.

After Mass Follow-Up

What runner leaps up from the dinner table and immediately begins a marathon? That's a sure road to indigestion or worse! Well, neither should we leap up from the Lord's table without giving ourselves an opportunity to digest what we've consumed.

The Eucharist is a lavish banquet, and it takes some digestion to really profit from it. Since it's too rich for us to absorb all at once, the church encourages us to take time to pray after Mass. As the *Catechism* points out, "prayer internalizes and assimilates the liturgy during and after its celebration" (par. 2655).

What better place to pray than the very church where you've just participated in the Mass? When you can, linger a little bit after the dismissal to be with the Lord and continue your thanksgiving. This isn't just my idea; the church recommends it in an official document called "On Holy Communion and the Worship of the Eucharistic Mystery outside of Mass." It reads: "In order to continue more surely in the thanksgiving that in the Mass is offered to God in an eminent way, those who have been nourished by Communion should be encouraged to remain for some time in prayer" (par. 25).

Social time with other members of the church is important, too. Since we're all members of Christ's body, we should be getting to know one another and enjoying each other's company either before or after Sunday Mass. But that's not incompatible with taking five or ten minutes for personal prayer after the last song. It helps if the entire parish can make an agreement to keep the church quiet after Mass. Fellowship can begin outside the sanctuary—in the vestibule, church hall, or parking lot. I know of a Catholic university that adopted this approach, and it's working beautifully. At the end of Mass, they turn the lights down low, and whoever needs to leave right away does so. Most people kneel down to pray for a few minutes and then proceed outside for coffee, fun, and sharing.

Prayerful follow-up to the Mass can also take place later at home. This might happen individually, as we find snippets of time for personal prayer, or as a family or other grouping of Catholics who have been to Mass that day. In my own family, we often go over the Scriptures right after dinner, when we're all gathered around the table. Again, with young children present, it's an imperfect experience. There's no guarantee that we'll actually finish reading the passages out loud. Sometimes the kids pay attention, and sometimes they're a million miles away. But we've seen enough fruit from our successes that we find it's worth the effort. And again, even our failures say something to the kids and to the Lord.

I was once comforted by a priest who told my wife and me that the attempt to pray is itself prayer. The attempt to love is itself love. I hang onto this thought whenever we experience little recollection or satisfaction in our family prayers. God honors our intentions and efforts.

Keep Holy the Lord's Day

For the last hundred years, various popes have emphasized that there's more to Sunday, the day of the Lord, than simply going to church for an hour. Part of getting more out of the Mass involves making Sunday a day that is colored entirely by the joy of the Resurrection. It's a day to celebrate our victory in Christ!

The question is how to make this happen in our own lives. In *Dies Domini*, a wonderful letter written in 1998, John Paul II offers many valuable ideas on making the Lord's Day special. He begins by noting that in the Western world we no longer experience the week as six days and the Lord's Day; we now have five days and the weekend. Unfortunately, most Catholics are influenced by society's weekend mentality—namely, to use Saturday and Sunday for catching up on things like yard work and laundry.

But Christians at times must take stands that could be considered countercultural. Regarding Sunday, Catholics are bound to avoid heavy or "servile" work. The church doesn't spell out precisely what falls into this category but simply directs us to avoid labor that one might consider drudgery. At my house, this leads to all kinds of debates.

"Do the dishes," I tell my daughter.

"But Dad, we're not supposed to work on Sunday..."

"Do you eat on Sunday?"

"Yes."

"Well then, you do dishes on Sunday."

Some things just have to be done daily. On the other hand, there are certain major projects, like scrubbing the bathrooms or cleaning out the garage, that my family doesn't do on Sunday unless it is a matter of dire necessity.

There are also positive ways we try to mark Sunday out as special. We sometimes spend a little extra time praying together—singing, reading selections from a saint's life, watching a video with a Christian message. We have a nicer than usual meal, complete with dessert. More importantly, we try to implement the Holy Father's directive to view Sunday as a day for contemplating God's goodness and gifts.

Like most people, I have a to-do list as long as my arm. On Sundays, though, I put the list away and look at what *God* has accomplished for me, for those I love, for the whole human race. This gives the whole day a particular quality of thanksgiving, which is a way of extending the Eucharist. Church teaching encourages this approach:

> Union with Christ, to which the sacrament itself is directed, is not to be limited to the duration of the celebration of the Eucharist; it is to be prolonged into the entire Christian life, in such a way that the Christian faithful, contemplating unceasingly the gift they have received, may make their life a continual thanksgiving....
>
> *EUCARISTICUM MYSTERIUM*, par. 38

Finally, it's altogether appropriate to do acts of service on the Lord's Day—for the poor, the lonely neighbor down the street, a faraway relative who'd be cheered by a phone call, the sick or elderly in the hospital or nursing home (see John Paul II, *Dies Domini*, par. 72). If we do this, we're responding to the special commissioning that the priest gives in the Roman rite: "The Mass is ended. Go in peace to love and serve the Lord." The word *Mass*—which is derived from *missa*, from the Latin word meaning dismissed—includes the idea of being com*mission*ed, sent out on mission. Following up the Mass by serving makes sense because the Mass is the sacrament of charity.

Adoration of the Blessed Sacrament

One kind of follow-up to Sunday Mass deserves special attention here. This is adoration of the Blessed Sacrament—times between Masses when we linger with the Lord in front of the reserved sacrament. In some parishes, adoration is organized around the clock, with people signing up for one-hour shifts. More informally, many Catholics simply stop at church to visit with the Lord for a few minutes during the course of the day.

Consecrated hosts are kept at church primarily so that Communion is always available to the sick and the dying. Having the Lord's bodily presence so available gives us all ample opportunity to respond in adoration and to be strengthened in our faith. The church insists, however, that adoration always be understood in connection with the Eucharistic liturgy. Basically, adoration is an opportunity to reflect on what happens at Mass, which is an event so profound that it needs to be digested through ongoing meditation. In adoration, we hold the Eucharist in a long moment of contemplation and assimilate more deeply the gifts we received there.

A good way to increase our appreciation for adoration is to participate in Benediction of the Blessed Sacrament. In this beautiful service which usually opens a prolonged solemn period of adoration, the priest removes a consecrated host from the tabernacle, places it in a magnificent holder called a monstrance, and lifts it up to bless the congregation.

The monstrance's traditional shape—a sunburst, with the host in the center of converging rays—is a visual commentary on the Body of Christ. It emerged against the background of the reign of Louis XIV, the powerful seventeenth-century French monarch known as the "Sun King." By linking the sun and the Eucharist—instead of King Louis or any human power—the monstrance proclaims that Jesus is the true "sun of righteousness" who has "healing in its wings" and breaks upon us like the "dawn ... from on high" (see Mal 4:2; Lk 1:78). Jesus alone is the King of Kings!

For me, adoration is kind of like sun bathing: I put myself in the presence of the Lord and allow myself to bask in the healthful rays of the sun of righteousness. I've spent many moments in adoration over the last twenty-five years and have received healing of some very significant wounds. The Lord has also used these times to guide me in some remarkable ways. It was in front of the Blessed Sacrament, for example, that I discovered my vocation to become a theologian.

I must also confess that there have been many times when my adoration has wandered off into daydreams, distractions, and even sleep! Not every moment before the Blessed Sacrament is glorious, I've discovered, but if you persevere, you *will* have moments when the Lord touches you profoundly. They make all the struggles worthwhile.

What to Do, What to Expect

People ask me, "But what do you *do* when you pray before the Blessed Sacrament?" First, let me point out what *not* to do. There are two extremes to avoid. At one end of the spectrum is hyper-busyness. This happens when people feel so uncomfortable with quiet that they fill up every minute of adoration with nonstop talking to God; this leaves no room for silent attentiveness to God's voice. Yet others think that it's inappropriate to do anything except be still and gaze on the Eucharist. The problem here is that most of us aren't equipped to walk in from our busy life and instantly focus. Our minds are everywhere but on the presence of the Lord.

So how does one pray before the Blessed Sacrament? Since Eucharistic adoration is essentially a matter of contemplating the Mass, everything that happens at Mass is appropriate to do during adoration. In fact, church documents on the subject teach that we should take the Mass as our guide.

Notice that at Mass, we don't jump into Communion right away. We prepare ourselves by repentance, listening to God's word in Scripture, offering praise in prayers like the *Gloria* and the Eucharistic Prayer. We intercede for the needs of all. Finally, we receive the Lord and rest in his presence, giving ourselves to him and enjoying a deep union with him.

Each of these types of prayer is suitable for our times before the Blessed Sacrament. Certainly, there's no obligation to always use them all or to follow the exact sequence in which they appear in the Mass. At the same time, our adoration should culminate as the Mass does, with simple resting in the arms of our Beloved.

Silently repeating a word or short phrase can be a great aid in keeping us focused as we gaze on the Lord. One great tradition in the church is to repeat the name of Jesus or the well-known Jesus Prayer: "Lord Jesus Christ, Son of God, have mercy on me." Also, certain Scriptures are especially effective in helping us recall that we're in the Lord's magnificent presence. One of my favorites is Psalm 46:10: "Be still, and know that I am God." Another is Psalm 63, which speaks of thirsting and pining for God as in "a dry and weary land" and goes on to evokes the joy of gazing on God "in the sanctuary" and being filled, as with a banquet (verses 1-8). This, of course, is truly what happens in adoration: it's a spiritual communion that fills our soul, as with a banquet.

It's thought-provoking, I think, to consider Church teaching on the different ways Communion can be received. Some people receive it sacramentally but not spiritually: they take the host on their lips without any preparation and therefore without any fruit; objectively, grace is received, but in vain. Other people prepare for Communion; their reception is sacramental and also spiritual.

Additionally, the Council of Trent identified a third kind of Communion which is spiritual but not sacramental. This is possible at times when, without being able to sacramentally receive the Lord's Body and Blood, you give yourself to Jesus and receive him spiritually. The church insists that the same fruit can be borne in spiritual Communion as in sacramental Communion, if people are properly disposed. I find it encouraging to remember this at the times when I'm prevented from getting to Mass and Communion.

Adoration is a wonderful moment of grace. This is true, too, for our non-Catholic brothers and sisters who love Jesus but can't receive the Eucharist because our churches are not one. I know of several such Christians who believe in the real presence of the Lord's Body and Blood in the Eucharist, adore him there, and experience wonderful blessings.

"I'm not getting anything out of Mass." Next time you hear someone say this—or fall into this way of thinking yourself—remember what the Church teaches about Christ's presence in the Eucharist. The good news is that he's really there, no matter how unsatisfactory the priest, the church, the music, and the liturgy may be. Nothing and no one can stop us from being in Jesus' presence to receive him and give ourselves to him. The bad news is, if we don't get anything out of Mass, it's our own fault. The responsibility rests on us.

So are we going to moan and complain when we don't find much support for our faith in those around us? Or are we going to take responsibility to pursue the Lord, like the woman with the hemorrhage? A whole crowd of faithless people didn't stop her from making her way to Jesus and touching the hem of his garment. Another gutsy petitioner, blind Bartimaeus, was surrounded by people who told him to shut up, but he cried out until Jesus heard and gave him what he asked (see Mk 10:46-52).

If we decide to pursue the Lord with everything we've got, we're going to find that he'll use us. Other folks will notice our faith, and they'll be inspired to exercise their faith, too. Eventually we'll see change in our family, neighborhood, parish, diocese, church. It's got to begin somewhere. Why not with me?!

Chapter Seven

Keeping a Pure Heart

Whether seasoned veterans or fresh recruits, all of Christ's disciples have something in common: we still sin. When the pressure is on, we sometimes crumble. "Why?" we ask ourselves in frustration. "Am I ever going to get over this? What can I do?"

It should encourage us to know that we're not alone in this ongoing struggle. Think about Peter, for example. Three years of living with Jesus, following him, watching him work miracles, and what does he say in the moment of testing? "I do not know the man" (Mt 26:72).

When, like Peter, we find ourselves wavering, it's important to realize that the problem isn't only in us. Objectively, we face a lot of pressure as Jesus' followers. Faith and baptism do not make us invulnerable to the forces that oppose Christ in this world.

The World, the Flesh, and the Devil

In the New Testament, three words sum up all the opposition that we encounter when we try to follow Jesus. These are the world, the flesh, and the devil.

"Love not the world." God created the world and everything in it, "and behold, it was very good" (Gn 1:31). He formed human beings in his image and paid the ultimate price to redeem them: "God so loved the world that he gave his only Son" (Jn 3:16). Obviously, this God-created world for which Jesus laid down his life is a great and precious good.

But the Bible also uses the word "world" to designate a prevailing social environment that's opposed to God. This is the meaning that underlies the warning, "Do not love the world or the things in the world.... For all that is in the world ... is not of the Father" (1 Jn 2:15-16).

Think about what makes our twenty-first-century world go round. It's that unholy trinity, the gods of sex, money, and power. With the media constantly promoting the idea that these are life's most important priorities, it's no wonder that these values affect our attitudes and choices. Let's face the fact that we're in a difficult situation. We're immersed in a worldwide culture that in many ways is contrary to the gospel.

Our adversary the devil. The ruler of this world—this system that's opposed to God—is Satan, or the devil. There are many different names for him, but more important than what you call him is what you know about him. The crucial fact is that he's a created spirit who chose to repudiate God. Out of hatred, he seeks to spoil God's work and to deceive God's children into following him into a doomed, hopeless existence.

People who think of the devil as a mythological fantasy or as a laughable character with a tail, pitchfork, and horns have a shocking surprise coming. In reality, the devil is a wily enemy with superhuman intelligence. Scripture tells us that Satan is a vicious adversary who "prowls around like a roaring lion, seeking some one to devour" (1 Pt 5:8). Only by God's power can we resist him, "for we are not contending against flesh and blood, but against the principalities, against the powers, against the world rulers of this present darkness, against the spiritual hosts of wickedness in the heavenly places" (Eph 6:12).

How does Satan win us over? One strategy is to insert thoughts into our minds. Often, these are so cleverly disguised that we don't recognize them as coming from outside ourselves. The diabolical suggestion, "You shouldn't believe God exists," pops up as, "I don't believe in God." It sounds like us talking, but it's really not. It's a temptation.

The devil also fogs our thinking and blinds us to the truth. Have you ever wondered why some people who see dramatic miracles of conversion or physical healing don't recognize God at work? Where does their blindness come from? And what keeps people from recognizing plain truths when the facts are right before them—for example, that an abortion destroys a human life? It's all the work of the one Jesus called a murderer, a liar, and the father of lies (see Jn 8:44).

Fighting the flesh. A common misconception has it that Christianity, and especially Catholicism, is hostile to the body and therefore encourages the repression of all natural bodily desires. This stems from a misunderstanding of what St. Paul means by "the flesh."

In the New Testament "the flesh" (see Romans 7 and 8) doesn't refer to the body. As created by God, the body with its natural desires is a great good. "The flesh," rather, is code language for the fallen nature inherited from our first parents, Adam and Eve. Through their rebellion against God, our humanity became somewhat warped and attracted towards destructive things. These downward tendencies sometimes get us off track, even after conversion to Christ. We are no longer slaves to sin, but some tug toward sin remains. This is what St. Paul calls the flesh.

Obviously, following the flesh leads to the sins of the flesh, gluttony and sexual immorality. Beyond that, though, is a more deadly pull toward bickering, jealousy, and hatred of other people (see Gal 5:19-21). At its heart, the flesh is essentially about selfishness—the drive to make "me" and not God the supreme center of the universe.

Christ has conquered the world, the flesh, and the devil, and his victory has made us free. Yet this total freedom will be fully realized in our lives only if we engage in a lifelong battle against these opponents. We have the Lord's power, and victory is guaranteed, if only we persist and don't lie down crying "uncle"!

Sin: A Few Basics

In the midst of this struggle, it's critical to remember that there's a difference between temptation and sin. Thoughts and attractions are not sins in themselves. Don't allow yourself to be fooled into guilty self-hatred just because you experience temptations.

Secondly, be aware that there's a difference between sin that destroys our relationship with God and sin that wounds it. All sin is bad, but not all sin is equal in terms of its seriousness and effects. "There is sin which is mortal," Scripture tells us. "All wrongdoing is sin, but there is sin which is not mortal" (1 Jn 5:16-17).

The Catholic Church distinguishes between these two types of sin—"mortal," or deadly, sin and "venial" sin, which some also call light sin. Mortal sin involves a deliberate decision to do something that we know is so gravely evil that it will rupture our relationship with God. When we decide to commit a lesser offense against God's law and don't intend by it to repudiate our relationship with God, that's venial sin (see *Catechism of the Catholic Church,* pars. 1854-1864).

No sin should ever be taken casually, however. St. Augustine says: "Do not despise these sins which we call 'light': if you take them for light when you weigh them, tremble when you count them" (quoted in the *Catechism,* par. 1863).

Sin may look good; it may promise a great payoff and even provide some initial pleasure. This is deceptive; the truth is that sin, whether mortal or venial, always leaves us wounded and desolate. Not only that: when individual members of Christ's body break God's law, no matter how "private" they consider their sin, the whole church is weakened. If we're only mildly disturbed about something that damages us and drains the lifeblood out of the whole church, then we need conversion. God hates all sin, and we ought to hate it, too.

Another truth about sin: it's not always a matter of committing a wrong; it can also mean neglecting to do what's right. If you fail to do your duty, that's sin. The most striking scriptural example appears in Matthew's last judgment scene (25:31-46). Why does the Lord tell some people, "Depart from me, you cursed," and not, "Come into the joy of my Father"? It's because of their sins of omission. Jesus even identified himself with the needy they failed to feed, welcome, clothe, and visit. Likewise, Jesus condemns the Pharisees for manipulating the rules so as to duck out of their obligation to support their aged parents (Mt 15:1-9).

When it comes to sins of omission, we all fall short. If you have any doubts about that, just reflect for awhile on the great commandment: Love the Lord your God with *all* your heart, soul, mind, and strength, and love your neighbor as yourself (see Mk 12:30-31).

Fortunately, none of us has to work out our own transformation. For this we have the Holy Spirit sent by Jesus as our counselor and advocate. You might think of him as a defense lawyer! The Holy Spirit does convict us of sin—not to torture us with guilt, but to draw us to the repentance that saves us from the sentence of death. If we reject sin and ask forgiveness, there's nothing that can't be cleansed and healed. But if we refuse and resist the Spirit's action, we commit the one unforgivable sin—the sin against the Holy Spirit, which blocks the way back to God (see Mt 12:31; *Catechism*, par. 1864).

Taking a Stand

What should we do when we discover sin in our lives? First, it's necessary to express sorrow or contrition for sin. People sometimes wonder, "What if I don't feel very sorry?" Fundamentally, the sorrow that leads to personal transformation isn't an emotion; it's a matter of decision. Maybe you still feel some inner attraction to the sin you want to reject. Don't worry. In time, your feelings will probably change. For now, God is pleased with your decision to repudiate the wrong you've done.

But apologizing to God isn't enough. Authentic repentance

has to involve taking an uncompromising stand against sin in your life. Saying "sorry" for an offense is meaningless if it's not backed by a sincere intention to avoid repeating it in the future. Knowing our own weakness, we can't guarantee that we'll never sin again, but true repentance requires a commitment to doing what we can to break sinful patterns and repair whatever damage we've done.

Another common concern about sorrow for sin has to do with motivation. A little honest self-examination will lead most of us to admit that our contrition is fueled by a number of motives. Am I sorry because I love God and know that he deserves better from me? Because I'm afraid of hell? Because I want to escape suffering the consequences of my sin? Instead of agonizing over our mixed motivations, we should trust that God will accept whatever motivation we're able to come up with, even if it's not quite perfect yet.

The story of the Prodigal Son strikes me as a good example of this. Here's a young man who rejects his father and blows his whole inheritance on loose living. Finally, when he's starving to death, he realizes that can get something to eat if he returns home. As he trudges back, he rehearses his little speech: "Father I've sinned against God and against you. I don't deserve to be called your son. Just let me be one of your hired servants" (see Lk 15:18-19).

Does it say that the prodigal was returning home out of sorrow for having hurt his father? It seems to me that his motives fall far short of pure love. But does the father care? He doesn't even listen to his son's speech! He runs out to greet him, opens his arms, and embraces his boy with great rejoicing.

Jesus told this parable to show that this is how God deals

with us. Sure, it's great if we can get to the place where we're sorry for our sins because we've disappointed a loving Father. But God's forgiveness doesn't depend on the purity of our motives. He rejoices over *any* movement in his direction. Not only that: as we head back towards the Father's house, he purifies our motivation so that eventually we care more about grieving him than about saving our skin.

Of course, deciding to forgive other people is a prerequisite for receiving forgiveness from God. "Forgive us our sins, as we forgive those who sin against us," we pray in the Our Father. In other words, when we harbor resentment against a brother or sister, we're cursing ourselves—calling God to treat us in the same way. Right after teaching the Our Father, Jesus drives this point home with a clear warning that God will not forgive anyone who fails to forgive others (see Mt 6:14-15). One way to put this teaching into practice is to cultivate the habit of asking one another's forgiveness.

Growing up, my family was like most others I knew. No one was ever able to look another in the eye and admit, "Forgive me, I was wrong." Simmering hurts and resentments were the result. But all those cleared up once we started applying this New Testament approach in my teenage years. What wonderful results came from discovering that when we blew it, we could simply go up to one another and say, "I'm sorry. Please forgive me"! My wife and I are continuing this liberating practice and teaching it to our children.

Live It Out!

Repentance begins with an inward decision, but it has to issue in an outward expression. That's because we're bodily creatures, not angels. Our very natures require that we express what's inside by the way we live. And as our words and actions change, this in turn deepens the transformation of our hearts.

Zacchaeus is a good biblical example of this change of heart that leads to change of life. Luke's Gospel introduces him as a "chief tax collector, and rich" (19:2). In first-century Palestine tax collectors were despised collaborators of the Roman oppressors. They worked on commission basis: the more they squeezed out of people, the more money they made. Tax collecting was brutal and heartless work, and apparently Zacchaeus was good at it.

Then one day Jesus comes to town and invites himself over to Zacchaeus's house. Moved by grace, the little tax collector is changed on the spot. He greets Jesus' words with joy, receives him warmly, and expresses sincere repentance by taking a radical new approach: "Lord, the half of my goods I give to the poor; and if I have defrauded any one of anything, I restore it fourfold" (Lk 19:8).

This is exactly the kind of visible change that John the Baptist demanded of those who came to him for baptism. He didn't exactly mince his words: "You brood of vipers! Who warned you to flee from the wrath to come? Bear fruits that befit repentance" (Lk 3:7-8). Asked what to do, John made some very practical suggestions. If you have two cloaks, give one to someone who has none; share your food; stop your robbing and extorting.

For us, too, such expressions of repentance help break our attachments to sin. Like medicine, they're not punitive measures but rather instruments of healing.

Pray, Fast, Give Alms, Endure

Scripture and the Church Fathers insist especially on three classic aids to effective repentance. These are prayer, fasting, and almsgiving.

Praying transforms our minds and hearts. As we read and reflect on God's word, the misguided thinking that leads us to sin is set right. We learn to see more clearly, to cherish the things that are truly valuable. Through prayer, we come to understand and believe the truth.

During my single days, I experienced just such a change of thinking with regard to an annoying roommate. Even though he was a brother in the Lord, his habits and ideas really irritated me. Frankly, I just couldn't stand this guy. Then one day in prayer, I felt that the Lord was saying to me, "I want you to pray for this person every day." I reacted with overjoyed relief. "Great! I'll pray that he'll be changed!" But I hadn't gotten it quite right, as the Lord proceeded to make clear: "No, I want you to pray in thanksgiving for the great creation that this person is—for his gifts, talents, and sincerity."

I accepted the challenge and began spending several minutes a day thanking God for my roommate. Before long my heart was changed! My attitude took a hundred-eighty degree turn, and I began to genuinely appreciate this person. Praying according to God's mind instead of my own made all the difference.

Fasting is also a powerful way to break our attachment to sin. The most common type of fast has to do with food—giving it up completely for a few hours or a day, or voluntarily depriving ourselves of some favorite food. (The choice is obvious for my sister-in-law, who has a poster that reads, "Chocolate is not a matter of life or death. It's much more serious than that.")

As mentioned earlier, we can also fast from media input. Most of us are stuffed to overflowing with the thoughts, sounds, and images received from television, radio, newspapers, CDs, and the internet. It's very salutary to take an occasional break from this barrage! It can also give you more time for prayer. Take the time you would have spent in front of the TV and put it into prayer instead, and you'll see some powerful transformations in your life.

Almsgiving furthers conversion because it provides a positive way to break the pattern of sin. Sin is an offense against charity; it undermines the love we owe God and other people. But when we share our resources through almsgiving, we repair the wrong we've done and demonstrate that our repentance is sincere. As the Bible says, "Love [charity] covers a multitude of sins" (1 Pt 4:8).

Notice that almsgiving, too, works well with fasting. You'll have more to give if you cut back on things like going to the movies, eating out, and buying the latest gadget. Fast from things like this once in a while, and give the money to the poor. It's a phenomenal way to change your heart and alleviate other people's suffering.

Prayer, fasting, and almsgiving are disciplines that we choose to deal with our personal sin and break its hold on us. But in the course of everyday life, we also encounter many *unchosen trials* that produce the same results. In fact, the Catholic Church teaches that the most powerful form of penance is "above all the patient endurance of the cross we must bear" (*Catechism,* par. 1460). To lovingly accept these sufferings that are beyond our control, to raise them up to God with love is a transforming sacrifice of praise.

Often when I run up against one of these unchosen sufferings, I'm inspired by this thought from St. John Vianney, the nineteenth-century French pastor known as the Curé of Ars. Whenever duty requires us to do something we dislike, he counsels, "Let's say to God, 'My God, I offer this to you in honor of the moment when you died for me.'" That puts everything in perspective and strengthens my resolve to accept whatever discipline the Lord knows I need.

Special Moments for Repentance

Examination of conscience. The church encourages us to make a nightly review of each day's events to determine how we may have missed the mark. This prayerful self-reflection is a healthy discipline that helps us identify our weaknesses and open ourselves to God's transforming grace. Many Catholics find it convenient to make their examination of conscience just before going to bed. "Ok, Lord, I blew it here.... I shouldn't have said that. I'm sorry. Please forgive me..."

This regular review can also help us to identify "occasions of sin"—that is, persons, things, or situations that put us in spiritual jeopardy. For example, some people fall into greedy or lustful thoughts through watching certain television shows. If they really want to fight those sinful tendencies, they need to stop plopping themselves down in front of the TV, or at least change the channel. After all, you can't blame God for letting you fall into a pit if you walk up to the edge and lean over!

Making a daily examination of conscience is a powerful aid to repentance. Done over an extended period of time, it makes you aware of patterns of sin and areas of weakness that require special attention.

I've also found it helpful to reflect on Scripture passages that describe how followers of Christ are called to live—the Sermon on the Mount, for example (Mt 5-8), and Romans 12-15, which provides specifics about various duties of Christians. My favorite is 1 Corinthians 13, St. Paul's famous description of love. As I read through verses 4 to 8, I substitute my name for the word "love." The very first sentence always nails me: "Marcellino is patient and kind." There are certain occasions of the sin of impatience I can't avoid—like my five children, for instance! But examining myself against Scriptures like 1 Corinthians 13 reminds me to keep fighting the good fight.

Penitential Fridays. All Christians are obliged to honor the Lord's death. From the earliest days of the Church, Catholics have done this in a regular, communal way by observing each Friday as a day of fasting and penance. In some countries, church law requires Catholics to abstain from meat on Fridays; in countries like the U.S., this is required during Lent only.

Many Catholics are unaware of this, since this is seldom mentioned from the pulpit. But whether we abstain from meat or choose some other way to express sorrow for the sin that led Jesus to the cross, we all need to recover the powerful discipline of a weekly commemoration of Christ's death for us (see *Catechism*, par. 1438).

Liturgical helps. For Catholics, Lent is an entire season of repentance, a time for examining ourselves individually and as a people in order to grow in holiness. The Eucharist includes a penitential rite at the beginning of every celebration; it provides an opportunity to recall our sins and ask the Lord's forgiveness. Confession—also known as penance or reconciliation—is the sacrament that's specifically directed to dealing with sins committed after baptism. It's one of the most effective tools in our struggle to keep a pure heart.

The Good Medicine of Confession

We have the sacrament of confession because the Lord gave it to us. On the day he rose from the dead, according to John 20:22, Jesus gave this authority to the apostles by breathing on them and saying, "Receive the Holy Spirit. If you forgive the sins of any, they are forgiven; if you retain the sins of any, they are retained." The bishops of the Catholic Church, as successors of the apostles, have been given this awesome authority for the good of God's people, and they have shared this authority with their priestly assistants.

The Lord didn't institute this sacrament because he wanted to make things difficult for us! Going to confession *is* painful sometimes, but it's a priceless gift. In the sacrament of reconciliation, we meet Christ in the person of the priest. We receive not only forgiveness, but a new outpouring of the Spirit to strengthen us against further sin. You might think of every confession as a new Pentecost.

I need help to change, so I go to confession as often as I can.

How often is it required? Church law is very minimal: a Catholic who has committed serious, or mortal sin must receive the sacrament of penance at least once a year. But more frequent confession, even of only venial sin, is highly recommended. Why wait till the situation is grave before making use of such life-giving medicine?

What if a person wants to go to confession but doesn't remember how? "I don't know what to do.... I've forgotten the words...." Well, relax. The rite of confession is very informal. We confess our sins as best we can, in our own words; then we ask forgiveness and express our sorrow either in our own words or in a formal prayer like the Act of Contrition. To make the experience as easy as possible, the church also gives us the option of confessing face to face or from behind a screen to insure anonymity.

The priest stands in the place of Christ, the Divine Physician. We confess our sins to him not so that we can be humiliated but so that he can understand our condition and prescribe appropriate medicine. That medicine is what's called the penance, and it can include prayer, fasting, and almsgiving.

Now, some priests are better at dispensing this medicine than others. Some are skilled and creative. Others aren't very good either at counseling or at prescribing suitable penances. For this and other reasons, the church has always encouraged us to choose the priest we feel most comfortable with. If that's not our parish priest, then we can confess our sins to a priest from somewhere else. It is helpful, though, to have a regular confessor—a priest who can get to know us and therefore give more personalized counsel.

And what if the only priest available isn't such a great spiritual guide? Then remember, first of all, that Christ always meets us in the priest; his presence doesn't depend on the confessor's abilities. Also, confession doesn't have to be a great spiritual counseling session. It's wonderful when it happens, but even without this dimension, the sacrament is powerful and brings results. Finally, spiritual counseling doesn't have to be given in confession by a priest. Many laypeople or non-ordained religious can provide effective spiritual direction.

Examination of conscience, confession, Fridays, Lent, the penitential rite at Mass—all these things help us to pursue conversion as the *Catechism* says we should: not as a onetime event but as "an uninterrupted task for the whole Church" (par. 1428). If this sounds like a burden, just remember that it's all about casting off chains and weights and having wounds healed! Ongoing repentance truly creates a lifestyle of joy and freedom.

The apostle Peter entered into this lifestyle after his threefold denial of Christ. He repented, and so he continued to grow. Some thirty years later, when the pressure came on again, Peter greeted the moment with joy. "Yes, I know Christ," he was proud to say, "and I'm ready, willing, and able to give my life for him."

Like Peter in his early stage, we're weak and imperfect disciples, but the Lord will strengthen us, purify us, and help us to become saints, as he helped Peter. That's our objective, and daily repentance is the way through which we'll accomplish it. It's hard work but well worth the effort, because the joy produced by holiness lasts forever.

Chapter Eight

Mary and the Saints

Everyone knows that saints have a prominent place in Catholic life. We take saints' names for our children, schools, and churches. We have statues, medals, and scapulars of the saints. We invoke certain saints as special patrons of particular areas of life.

Of course, there are abuses. It's one thing to ask St. Anthony's help for finding a lost object, but the approach of my Italian grandfather's generation is another matter: in his family, if the lost object didn't appear in a timely fashion, St. Anthony's statue was taken outside, turned upside down, and left in the rain. A more current example of this kind of thing is burying a plastic St. Joseph statue in your yard as a "guaranteed" way to sell your house.

Obviously, such superstitions should be rooted out wherever they appear. But abuses aside, many people are troubled by more fundamental questions about saints. Is it right to put certain men and women on a pedestal? And anyway, aren't we all saints?

Big and Small "S" Saints

To be sure, we *are* all saints. In the New Testament, the word "saint," meaning holy one, is used to refer to anyone who has come to faith in Christ and been baptized (for example, see 2 Cor 1:1; Eph 1:1; Phil 1:1). In fact, the white garment given us in baptism is a graphic illustration of the purity that is ours when we "put on Christ." But the holiness received in baptism is like a mustard seed that needs to take root and grow. The canonized—or "capital S"—saints allowed that process to come to completion.

The saints were made out of flesh and blood, not plastic. Like us, they had their faults. Look at David, the Old Testament king. His passion for God was admirable, but his passion for another man's wife led to adultery and murder (2 Sam II). Read any good biography of a saint, and you'll find human characteristics that are easy to identify with.

Personally, I like saints who had a good sense of humor, like Teresa of Avila. Once, while traveling around sixteenth-century Spain, the wheel of the cart she was riding in hit a rock, pitching her into a puddle. Plastered with mud, she picked herself up and exclaimed, "God, if this is the way you treat your friends, no wonder you have so few of them!"

While most canonized saints are like us in many ways, the difference between them and us is their decision to take seriously two simple commandments: Love the Lord your God with all your heart, and love your neighbor as yourself (Mk 12:29-31). In doing this, the saints surrendered to God completely. They allowed his seed of holiness to grow into a great tree that gave shelter to everyone (Mk 4:32). They're like the good soil in Jesus' parable of the sower. They welcomed the seed and didn't let it wither up or get choked out by thorns and thistles. They tended it until it bore fruit—"thirtyfold and sixtyfold and a hundredfold" (Mk 4:20).

The saints are the folks who didn't just cry, "Lord, Lord," but who actually did the will of the heavenly Father (see Mt 7:21). In the great race of life, they're the ones who went for the gold. They weren't content to stumble their way through the race and finish whenever: they ran to win! Now, from the other side of the finish line, they urge us on to do the same. The awesome accomplishment of the saints is nicely summed up by the philosopher Peter Kreeft in these words: "The saints are greater conquerors than Alexander the Great. He merely conquered the world. They conquered themselves."

Honor the Lord, Honor His Works

Another question that troubles many Christians: Doesn't honoring the saints detract from Christ? Doesn't it usurp the worship that's due to him alone?

Catholic teaching on this point echoes the Bible. The first commandment says, "You shall have no other gods before me" (Ex 20:3). Only God is worthy of adoration. Notice, though, that a few verses later, the same God who commands us to *worship* him alone commands us to *honor* our parents: "Honor your father and your mother" (Ex 20:12).

As this indicates, there's no competition between worshiping the Lord and honoring the people he's established as his instruments and our authorities. In fact, the two responses are related.

This is evident throughout the Old Testament. God alone receives worship, but anyone connected with him is due honor. God's people bow down before priests, prophets, and kings; homage paid to such figures isn't seen as idolatrous, because it's essentially directed to the God whom they represent. Even *things* connected with God are given reverence. The ancient Israelites honor the Ark of the Covenant, which holds the Ten Commandments, and the sacred vessels used in the sacrifices. They bow before the Temple. All these things are worthy of honor because they're connected with the worship of God.

The fourth-century bishop St. Epiphanius said "He who honors the Lord honors also the holy vessel. He who dishonors the Lord also dishonors the vessel." Specifically, he was speaking of Mary, but, to a lesser degree, all the saints are God's dwelling and therefore worthy of honor. So honoring Mary and the saints doesn't detract from God. Because they show forth his power, honoring them glorifies him.

Taking my cue from the last part of Psalm 48, I sometimes think of the saints as strong and beautiful towers in God's holy city, Jerusalem. In fact, I take the following verses as an encouragement to honor the saints:

> Walk about Zion, go round about her,
> number her towers,
> consider well her ramparts,
> go through her citadels;
> that you may tell the next generation
> that this is God,
> our God for ever and ever.
> He will be our guide for ever.
>
> PSALM 48:12-14

Seeing the saints, we see God's work. Sinners like us, they reached the heights of virtue thanks to God's action in their lives. Now his glory shines through them, revealing the riches of Christ and drawing us to fall more deeply in love with God.

Mary, the Greatest "Great Lady" of All

Scripture gives us a special mandate to honor Mary. She is both queen of the holy nation and mother of the family we call the church.

Mary's role as queen makes sense in light of the powerful role played by the mother of the king in the Old Testament. Known as the Great Lady, the queen mother was the most important woman in the kingdom of Judah, even more important than the senior wife in the king's harem. She was seen as specially privileged, divinely chosen out of all the wives of the previous king to bring the current king, the "anointed one," into the world.

The first Great Lady is Bathsheba, King Solomon's mother. Notice the way Solomon treats her when she comes into his presence: "The king rose to meet her, and bowed down to her; then he sat on his throne, and had a seat brought ... and she sat on his right" (1 Kgs 2:19). Solomon gives no one else this royal treatment.

The Great Lady also has a special role of intercession. People desiring favors from the king seek her help first. When, for example, Bathsheba comes to Solomon to pass along just such a petition, Solomon responds, "Make your request, my mother; for I will not refuse you" (1 Kgs 2:20). In this particular story, because Bathsheba's request threatened Solomon's claim on the throne, things don't turn out well for the petitioner. Even so, the incident indicates that normally, kings were disposed to grant their mothers' requests.

The importance of the Great Lady can be seen, too, in the fact that 1 and 2 Kings never introduce any of the kings of Judah without also mentioning their mothers' names. One king even deposes his mother for being an idolatress (see 1 Kgs 15:13). Apparently, to be the Great Lady meant more than being the biological mother of the king; it was a matter of exemplifying the spiritual values of the nation. Another unworthy Great Lady demonstrates the power of the office by taking over the kingdom, executing claimants to the throne, and ruling for a number of years (2 Kgs 11:1-3).

This insistence on the status, privilege, and power of the Great Lady lies behind the figure of the new and greatest Lady, Mary. Elizabeth grasped this connection when Mary, who had conceived the Messiah in her womb, came to pay her a visit. That's why she exclaimed, "Who am I, that the mother of my Lord should come to me?" (see Lk 1:43).

Mary's unique role is also evoked in the book of Revelation's vision of a woman who appears in the heavens and then gives birth to a child. She is "clothed with the sun, with the moon under her feet, and on her head a crown of twelve stars" (12:1). Who is this woman? She is at the same time the church and Mary, the queen mother and Great Lady.

If the mother of the Old Testament king was to be honored, doesn't it then make sense to honor the mother of the Messiah in the New Testament? And since the Great Lady had a role of intercession in the Old Testament kingdom, why wouldn't she have one in the New?

An additional reason why Mary is especially worthy of honor: because she's mother of the King, she's also mother of the family to which we belong. We're brothers and sisters of Christ.

We're members of the church, which is called the body of Christ. If Mary is Christ's mother, then she's ours as well.

Our duty toward Mary is spelled out in the fourth commandment: "Honor your father and your mother." Interestingly, this commandment is the first to include a promise: do this, says the Lord, "that your days may be long in the land which the Lord your God gives you" (Ex 20:12). Honoring Mary is more than a duty. It's a pleasure and a joy; it's the way to an abundant life in the kingdom of God.

Choose Your Role Models!

The Second Vatican Council took up the question of how to honor Mary in a way that's most pleasing to God. Without diminishing the importance of other forms of piety, the Council emphasized *imitation* as the mainstay of Marian devotion (*Lumen Gentium* 67). Mary is given to us as a model, and the principal way to honor her is to imitate her virtues.

This is true of the saints as well. In fact, St. Paul says, "Be imitators of me, as I am of Christ" (1 Cor 11:1; see also Phil 3:17). He's not being arrogant; he's simply aware that people need models who can show them the way to fruitful discipleship.

In the saints, we have a wide variety of models of holiness. There are saints from all walks of life, of all conceivable temperaments, and from various historical epochs. With so many saints to choose from, each of us can easily find a role model. Children can look to St. Dominic Savio, the child saint. Dominic loved Jesus so much that he boldly requested permission to make his First Communion earlier than the customary age. Inspired by his example, my oldest daughter was begging for Communion early, too! Moms can be encouraged by Mother Mary who was herself a simple housewife. And we can't forget St. Monica who prayed long and hard for her wayward son, Augustine, who specialized in rebellion, sexual license, and cult involvement. Dads can look to St. Joseph. Political leaders can turn to St. Louis, king of France and St. Thomas More, chancellor of the realm under Henry VIII.

Reading biographies of such heroes is a great source of inspiration. In my house, we simply follow the liturgical calendar, with its regular progression of saints' days. I have a book that provides a short description of each saint, as he or she is commemorated in the calendar; I read this after dinner on the appropriate day.

Our family observes some saints' days with special festivity. Early on in our marriage, my wife and I made a decision not to name our children based on the latest fashion. Instead, we determined to name our children after saints who would be a special role model and intercessor for each child. As a result, we have a child named after St. Anthony and St. Francis; another after St. John the Baptist and St. Marcellino, a Roman who gave his life for Christ around the year 300; another after the Blessed Mother and St. Claire; another—Cristina Joy—in honor of Christ, who was anointed with the Holy Spirit of gladness; and another after St. Nicholas, the great saint of generosity who is linked with Christmas. So, besides a birthday, each person in our family has a "nameday" that is observed with appropriate festivities.

Following Mary's Footsteps of Faith

When it comes to imitation, the amazing thing about Mary is that she's a model for us all. Faith, faithfulness, surrender to God—these characteristics of hers are crucial for all Christ's disciples. Mary's example of faith stands out especially clearly in the Gospels of Luke and John.

"Blessed are you who believed that what was spoken to you by the Lord would be fulfilled" (Lk 1:45, NAB). This is the very first Beatitude in Luke's Gospel, and it is uttered by Elizabeth in praise of Mary. Earlier, Luke described the scene where God's word comes to Mary and announces that her whole life is going to have to change. Most likely, Mary had been planning to be an ordinary Jewish housewife with a big bunch of kids. Now she learns that God has other plans. Mary's question—"How will this be?"—is answered in a way that would leave most of us asking more questions, but Mary accepts the angel's message with a simple yes. "Let it be to me according to your word" (Lk 1:38).

In faith, Mary keeps God's word in her heart and ponders it (see Lk 2:19, 51). This makes her a model of a good pray-er, a contemplative who meditates on God's awesome deeds without necessarily understanding them fully right away. This is one reason I like to spend time with Mary by saying the rosary and meditating on the mysteries of Christ's birth, death, and resurrection. I can't imagine a better prayer partner.

Mary's faith is also highlighted toward the beginning of John's Gospel, in the story of the wedding feast of Cana. Because she believes that Jesus can do anything, she tells the servants to "do whatever he tells you" (Jn 2:5). Turning water into wine is the first "sign," or miracle, that John reports, and it begins Jesus' public ministry. As that ministry ends on the cross and all the apostles but one have fled, who is standing there but Mary? She's the model of faithfulness in the midst of trial (see Jn 19:26).

In a sense, Mary didn't do anything special. She didn't produce a lot of books or give talks that touched thousands of people or do the types of things on which overachievers base their self-worth. Mary simply accepted her part in God's plan and said "yes" to the Lord, not just once but again and again. She teaches me that all the Lord requires is that I say "yes," day in and day out.

Because Mary sought nothing for herself, she's also the model of perfect humility. Looking away from herself and only to God, she now reigns as queen of the kingdom where "the last will be first, and the first last" (Mt 20:16). Mary humbled herself, like the lowly child whom Jesus once held up as an example for his disciples (see Mt 18:1-4). For this reason we exalt her as supreme among all creatures, the "greatest in the kingdom of heaven" (Mt 18:4).

I'm inspired by Mary's humility, but I'm comforted, too. When I think of her *Magnificat*, that great song of praise in which she deflects all glory from herself and directs it back to the Lord, it gives me another reason for confidence about honoring Mary and the saints. Because of their humility, whatever honor is paid to them is relayed right to God. Ultimately, he gets all the glory.

The "One Mediator" and His Work

Though many Christians might concede that it's fine to use Mary and the saints as guides along the pathway to discipleship, they balk at the idea of praying to the saints. "Isn't that, well, idolatrous?" they wonder. "Isn't it wrong to pray to anyone but God?"

First of all, it's important to note that the word "pray" doesn't refer to the adoration that is due to God alone. It simply means "ask." Modern French conserves this meaning, and old English did too: "I pray thee, do not tarry...." When we pray to the saints, then, we're asking for help and not worshiping them.

We can, of course, go directly to Christ for help. As the Bible says, he is "the one mediator between God and men" (1 Tm 2:5). But, using this very Scripture passage to explain proper devotion to Mary (and, by extension, the saints), Vatican II emphasized that Mary's role as mother, helper, and intercessor "in no way obscures or diminishes this unique mediation of Christ, but rather shows its power" (*Lumen gentium*, par. 60).

Mary and the saints are members of Christ's body, the church. As such, they share in everything that Christ does, including his role as mediator. That's how it works with us, too. We're members of the Lord's body, so the Lord uses us to touch other people. When we pray and intercede for others, it's really the Lord praying and interceding through us.

Among the many members that make up the Body of Christ and exercise different functions in it, Mary has a wonderfully unique role that God has chosen for her. She's the mother of the entire Body. This gives her a very special share in Jesus' priesthood and his role of Mediator. Like the Great Lady and queen mother, Mary has a special role and ministry of intercession which is a sharing in the ongoing work of her Son.

Hebrews 7:25 says that Christ always lives to make intercession for us. He remembers us even now, as he sits at the Father's right hand enjoying his glory. Now, if this is true of the Head of the Body, wouldn't it be true of his members? Wouldn't the members of the body who have finished the race want to imitate their Head's continual intercession for us? "I want to spend my heaven doing good on earth," St. Thérèse of Lisieux said before she died. I think this expresses the sentiment of all the saints. Caught up in loving Christ, they can't stop loving us. Now having taken up residence in the Father's house, they pray for us until we, too, are safely home.

My Prayer Partners, the Saints

I think of the saints as prayer partners and turn to them for spiritual support, as I often turn to other Christians around me. The Bible tells me that a person's faith level has something to do with what they can expect to receive from prayer. Consequently, I know that I'd be in a very serious predicament if I had to rely just on my own faith when I'm in need. That's why I usually ask people who have more faith than I do to support me in prayer. If I have a bodily illness and someone with a special healing ministry comes to town, I go to be prayed with by that person. I do the same with Mary and the saints.

Mary is the model of faith. Who better to pray for me when my own faith needs bolstering? I'm working on it, but my faith isn't yet the mustard-seed, mountain-moving size! Until it is, I need faith-filled intercessors. This is scriptural, too. Referring to the Old Testament prophet Elijah, the letter of James points out that "the prayer of a righteous man has great power in its effects" (5:16). Well, since the saints are fully righteous—"the spirits of just men made perfect" (Heb 12:23)—their prayer is powerfully effective. I seek it as often as I can!

No Catholic is strictly obliged to make prayer to Mary and the saints part of their personal devotional life, but it will always be part of mine. One reason is that I've experienced the effects of their intercession again and again. Mary's assistance figured prominently in God's granting one of the most heartfelt prayers of my life.

About the time that my brother and I both came to deeper faith in Christ, my mom was struggling with a life-threatening disease. The two of us made a pledge to pray a decade of the rosary together every day, inviting Mary to pray with us for our mom's recovery. We kept this up every day for two years, without seeing anything change. Then, all of a sudden, my mother experienced an incredible breakthrough. It was as if all that intercessory prayer had been stored up behind a dam which had finally broken! Later, when mom had a relapse of this illness, she herself sought the help of the Blessed Mother. Again, she experienced God touching her through Mary's prayers, and she was out of danger. She has been symptom-free now for many years.

I'm sold on having Mary and the saints as my prayer partners. What sense would it make to overlook such powerful help?

They Follow the Lamb

Like many people, I used to wonder how the saints could hear our prayers. Only God is present everywhere. Only he can hear everyone's prayers at once. The saints are human beings. They've been glorified at God's right hand, but they're not everywhere at once, so how can they hear us?

If you looked at their human nature alone, you'd have to conclude that the saints can't hear us. But because the saints are glorified members of Christ, who is both God and man, they aren't bound by the limitations of their nature. Addressing this question back in the fourth century, St. Jerome highlighted the saints' intimate sharing in Christ by quoting Revelation 14:4: "It is these who follow the Lamb wherever he goes." By grace, where Christ is, the saints are, too. Somehow, he conveys the information they need to pray and intercede for us. How exactly does this happen? We don't know. We just know it works, and so we do it. I don't know how electricity works either, but I flip the switch and enjoy the lights anyway.

Because the saints live as members of Christ's body, asking them for help is nothing like the occult practice, forbidden by Scripture, of consulting the dead. We can see this in the story of King Saul's consulting a medium to conjure up the spirit of Samuel (see 1 Sm 28). Saul disobeyed by seeking guidance independently of God. Turning to the saints is just the opposite. It's something we do in Christ: as members of Christ's body, we ask our glorified brothers and sisters to pray for us. The connection is established by God and draws us ever closer to him and to one another.

When I was a young Catholic, I thought that only a chosen few were called to be saints. I put those saints on pedestals and settled for a lukewarm Christian life. "I can't hope to achieve that kind of holiness," I told myself. "I'll put a few dollars in the collection basket, try to stay away from mortal sin, and hope to squeak through the door at the end."

When I finally understood the truth, it came as truly good news. God didn't want me to settle for "good enough"! He wanted me to be among those heroes I admired so much. Furthermore, he had provided everything I needed to rise to the heights of holiness.

This is God's plan for each of us. He calls us to be not just sheep but disciples who can serve as models for others. "Don't hide your light under a bushel basket," Christ tells us. "Let it flame up and burn brightly to give light to all" (see Mt 5:15-16). How are we going to do this? By hanging around with the saints, keeping their company, seeking their intercession. By God's grace, their holiness will rub off on us.

"The only tragedy in life is not to become a saint," said the French Catholic writer Léon Bloy. Let's decide not to allow our lives to come to such a tragic and mediocre end. Rather, "surrounded by so great a cloud of witnesses," the saints, "let us also lay aside every weight, and sin which clings so closely, and let us run with perseverance the race that is set before us" (Heb 12:1).

Instead of just plodding along, let's run to win!

Additional Resources

This book, *Exploring the Catholic Church*, accompanies Dr. Marcellino D' Ambrosio's video cassette series of the same name.

He designed the video series as an immediate follow-up for Catholic Alpha, which is an evangelistic program that introduces people to Christianity. Although the series is primarily for those with little knowledge of the Catholic Church, many practicing Catholics find it very practical and inspiring.

For information about the video series or about Catholic Alpha, please contact:

Catholic Evangelisation Services
PO Box 333
St Albans
Herts AL2 1EL

Tel: 01727 823803
Fax: 01727 822837
e-mail: info@catholicevangel.org
Website: www.catholicevangel.org

Alternatively:

- In Australia, e-mail John Clements at clements@adam.com.au
- In New Zealand, fax Pat Clegg on (04) 566 5786
- In South Africa, e-mail Renato Acquisto at avmark@icon.co.za

Additional Resources

[illegible] are Catholic programmes [illegible] [illegible]
[illegible] [illegible].

[illegible] as an [illegible] [illegible] [illegible] [illegible] [illegible], which [illegible] people to [illegible]. Although the series is primarily for those who are [illegible] in the Catholic Church or [illegible] Catholic [illegible] [illegible].

For information about the [illegible] [illegible] [illegible] [illegible], please contact:

Catholic Information Services
[illegible]
St Albans
Herts AL[illegible]

Tel: [illegible]
[illegible]
and [illegible]
[illegible]

[illegible]

[illegible]

[illegible]

[illegible]